# Love, Twists & Blissful Kisses

von Hortense Ullrich

W0174533

PONS GmbH
Stuttgart

# PONS

## Love, Twists & Blissful Kisses

von Hortense Ullrich
Englisch von Brian Melican

basierend auf den Geschichten „Bliss Comes with a Kiss" und „Ein Kuss, ein Tor" von
Hortense Ullrich aus den Büchern:

„Summer, Sun & Holiday Love" © 2005
„Liebe, Schuss, Elfmeterkuss" © 2010
by Planet Girl (Thienemann Verlag GmbH) Stuttgart/Wien

Auflage A1 $^{6\ 5\ 4\ 3}$ / 2018 2017 2016 2015

© **PONS GmbH, Rotebühlstraße 77, 70178 Stuttgart, 2010**
**www.pons.de**
**E-Mail: info@pons.de**
**Alle Rechte vorbehalten.**

**Englische Überarbeitung, Annotationen und Übungen:** Brian Melican
**Redaktion:** Canan Eulenberger-Özdamar
**Logoentwurf:** Erwin Poell, Heidelberg
**Logoüberarbeitung:** Sabine Redlin, Ludwigsburg
**Einbandillustration:** Birgit Schössow
**Einbandgestaltung:** Daniel Müller, Stuttgart
**Sprecherin/Tonaufnahmen:** Nicola Barber, New York
**Layout:** one pm, Petra Michel, Stuttgart
**Satz:** Digraf.pl - dtp services

Printed in the EU.
**ISBN: 978-3-12-010023-2**

# INHALTSANGABE

## Bliss Comes With a Kiss

Jojo hat Liebeskummer. Von einem Tag auf den anderen meldet sich ihr
Freund Sven nicht mehr bei ihr. Warum bloß? Jojo hat keine Ahnung, ihre
beste Freundin Lucilla auch nicht. Deren Vorschlag: immer schön locker
bleiben, Sven vergessen und sich um einen passenden Ersatz kümmern.
Doch nichts läge Jojo ferner. Während die anderen Sommerferien und
Sonnenschein genießen, sperrt sich Jojo zu Hause ein … und grübelt – bis
Sven sich dann doch noch meldet und ihr ausrichten lässt, sie solle ihn
am nächsten Tag im Park treffen. Will er sie loswerden, auf übelste Weise
verlassen – oder hat er vielleicht etwas ganz anderes vor?

## The Football Pitch of Dreams

Für Sportmuffel Jojo gibt es nichts Schlimmeres, als sich ein Fußball-
spiel anschauen zu müssen – die anstrengenden Verkupplungsversuche
ihrer besten Freundin Lucilla vielleicht ausgenommen. Aber zum Glück
ist Lucilla auch kein wirklicher Fußballfan und für sie gibt es nur einen
geeigneten Zeitvertreib, während die ganze Schule ihre Mannschaft beim
Spiel anfeuert: Ausschau halten nach möglichen Pärchen und diese dann
zusammenbringen – wenn nötig mit etwas Nachhilfe!
Mit der Beauty-Notfall-Ausrüstung in der Hand geht Lucilla auf das
unscheinbare Mauerblümchen Sara los, um deren Glück mit Mannschafts-
kapitän Oliver auf die Sprünge zu helfen. Auch für die widerwillige Jojo gibt
es eine wichtige Mission …

# AUFTRETENDE PERSONEN

### Jojo

Jojo ist chaotisch und tollpatschig – mit einem Wort: eine wandelnde Katastrophe. Und das hat sich inzwischen schon an anderen Schulen herumgesprochen. Die selbstbewusste Jojo kann aber in jeder Situation ganz schön Kontra geben und dafür lieben sie ihre beste Freundin Lucilla und ihr Freund Sven.

### Lucilla

Modisch und stilbewusst, immer mit Wechsel-T-Shirt und der Beauty-Notfall-Ausrüstung für alle Fälle unterwegs: Lucilla ist sofort dabei, wenn nette Jungs neue Freundinnen brauchen – auch wenn man ihnen erst ein wenig zu ihrem Glück verhelfen muss. Doch Lucilla lässt sich durch solche Kleinigkeiten nie stören und schwenkt ihren Zauberstab, bis alles so klappt, wie sie sich das vorstellt.

## Bliss Comes With a Kiss

### Sven

Auch wenn Jojos verrückte Aktionen die Beziehung mit ihrem Freund Sven schon auf die eine oder andere Probe gestellt haben, hält er stets zu Jojo und lässt sich auch durch ihre Launen nie aus der Ruhe bringen.

### Flippi

Ihre jüngere Schwester Flippi würde Jojo mit einem Wort als „nervtötend" bezeichnen. Flippi gehört zu der Sorte Schwestern, die nie anklopfen, viel zu viel reden und sich in Dinge einmischen, die sie nichts angehen ... außerdem züchtet sie mit Leidenschaft Schnecken.

# The Football Pitch of Dreams

## Sara

Lucilla kann mit jüngeren Mädchen nicht viel anfangen - zumal man mit ihr an der Seite nicht gerade als cool gilt. Aber, ob sie will oder nicht, mit Sara muss sie ab und zu etwas unternehmen, da ihre Mütter befreundet sind. Auch Sara, für die Make-up ein Fremdwort ist, ist nicht gerade Lucillas größter Fan - sie findet sie oberflächlich und langweilig.

## Oliver

Oliver ist Kapitän der Fußballmannschaft von Jojos und Lucillas Schule und ein richtig süßer Typ, für den viele Mädchen schwärmen. Oliver aber interessiert sich für die mysteriösen Mädchen - auch wenn die nicht gerade immer im Mittelpunkt stehen.

Wie es sich für beste Freundinnen gehört, halten sich Lucilla und Jojo stets auf dem Laufenden - natürlich per SMS.

Daher findest Du an einigen Stellen im Text den einen oder anderen „Hilferuf" den eine von beiden der anderen durchschickt.

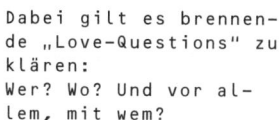

Dabei gilt es brennende „Love-Questions" zu klären:
Wer? Wo? Und vor allem, mit wem?

Beantworte die Fragen. Eine Liste mit SMS-Abkürzungen findest du auf S. 78 und die Lösungen ab S. 123.

Hortense Ullrich

# Bliss Comes With a Kiss

"No, I don't think you scared him away[1], Jojo." Lucilla shakes
her head. "Never! Not Sven! After all, he's been through enough
with you anyway[2]!"

"What's that supposed to[3] mean?" I ask, annoyed.

Lucilla looks at me wide-eyed. "Oh, come on, be honest[4]! Who
else would put up with you without complaining[5]?"

As Lucilla and I walk on, I think about what she has said. She's
right. The fact that Sven hasn't called me for two days and seems
to have disappeared into thin air[6] probably means nothing. We've
been together for ages[7], and Sven has the patience of a saint[8] with
me.

That's due to[9] his sense of humour, and my mum always says I'm
only bearable[10] if you have either a sense of humour or some pretty
strong sedatives[11]. How lucky I am to have Lucilla! I smile a big
smile at her. "You're right, Lucilla. I really don't have any reason
to panic!"

But Lucilla seems to have second thoughts[12]. "On the other hand …"
she says, thinking out loud[13].

• • • • • • • • •

1 **to scare sb. away** – *jdn. vergraulen*
2 **he's been through enough with you anyway** – *er hat ja schon genug mit dir durchgemacht*
3 **What's that supposed to mean?** – *Was soll das denn heißen?*
4 **honest** – *ehrlich*
5 **to complain** – *sich beklagen*
6 **to have disappeared into thin air** (Redewendung) – *wie vom Erdboden verschwunden sein*
7 **for ages** – *seit Ewigkeiten*
8 **patience of a saint** – *Engelsgeduld*
9 **due to sth.** – *wegen*
10 **bearable** – *erträglich*
11 **sedatives** – *Beruhigungsmittel*
12 **to have second thoughts** – *es sich anders überlegen*
13 **to think out loud** – *laut denken*

Racked with doubt¹, I stop dead in my tracks² and grab³ Lucilla's arm. "What?"

"What do you mean, 'what'?"

"You know, what do you mean by 'on the other hand'?"

"Oh, right, yeah …" Lucilla takes a deep breath. "Now don't get all worked up⁴, but …"

"I never get worked up!" I snap at her⁵.

"… if you think about all the expectations⁶ you've had of Sven until now," continues Lucilla, "you might be able to understand him if he did …"

"If he did what?" My voice almost breaks as I speak.

Lucilla shrugs⁷ her shoulders apologetically⁸. "You know, if he …"

"Dumped me⁹?" I cry, almost beside myself¹⁰. "Is that what you're trying to say?"

Lucilla is taken aback¹¹. "Oh no, of course not. I meant if he … if he … needed a break!" She smiles, relieved¹².

"A break?"

Lucilla nods¹³. "Yes, like a Jojo-free period."

"A Jojo-free period?" I mumble¹⁴ flatly. "It's the beginning of the end! And at the start of the holidays of all times¹⁵! Great!"

· · · · · · · · ·

1 **racked with doubt** - *von Zweifeln geplagt*
2 **to stop dead in one's tracks** (Redewendung) - *wie angewurzelt stehen bleiben*
3 **to grab** - *fassen, greifen, packen*
4 **to get (all) worked up** - *sich in etw. hineinsteigern*
5 **to snap at sb.** - *jdn. anschnauzen*
6 **expectation** - *Erwartung*
7 **to shrug (one's shoulders)** - *mit den Schultern zucken*
8 **apologetically** - *entschuldigend*
9 **to dump sb.** - *mit jdm. Schluss machen*
10 **beside oneself** - *außer sich*
11 **to be taken aback** - hier: *völlig perplex sein*
12 **relieved** - *erleichtert*
13 **to nod** - *(zustimmend) nicken*
14 **to mumble** - *murmeln, nuscheln*
15 **now of all times** - *ausgerechnet jetzt*

9

Lucilla puts her arm around me and tries to comfort[1] me. "It's OK, don't blame yourself.[2]"

We walk on towards the ice-cream parlour in silence. After a while, she asks me, "What did you say to him when you saw each other for the last time?"

I flinch[3]. "The last time? How can you say something like that, Lucilla?"

I just wanted to know what happened when you two … er … well, the last time you … I'm sorry, Jojo, I can't think of another way of saying it! What did you talk about?"

I sniffle[4] and shrug my shoulders. "I don't know."

"Come on, make an effort[5]. Think! Maybe you said something that …"

"… scared him off[6]?" I break down in tears[7].

Lucilla gives me a nudge[8]. "No, something that could help us out … something that could explain why he…"

I look at her despairingly[9]. "Go on, say it: something that could explain why he doesn't want to have anything to do with me anymore!"

Lucilla waves her hand dismissively[10]. "That's stupid! Stop thinking so negatively! Maybe he's just had an accident."

"You're not just saying that to make me feel better?"

· · · · · · · · ·

1 **to comfort sb.** – *jdn. trösten*
2 **to blame oneself** – *sich selbst die Schuld geben*
3 **to flinch** – *zucken*
4 **to sniffle** – *schniefen*
5 **Make an effort!** – *Streng dich an!*
6 **to scare sb. off** – *jdn. abschrecken, verschrecken*
7 **to break down in tears** – *in Tränen ausbrechen*
8 **nudge** – *Schubs*
9 **despairingly** – *verzweifelt*
10 **dismissively** – *abweisend*

"Not at all!" says Lucilla. "Maybe he really can't get in touch[1] with you right now."

I smile again and give Lucilla a grateful hug[2]. "You're right. That's so nice of you. That must be the reason why he hasn't called!" I keep walking along beside Lucilla[3], perfectly happy now. Yes, that must be it: Sven wouldn't leave me; he's probably just had an accident.

Suddenly, I stop dead in my tracks again. "An accident? Oh my God, Lucilla!"

Lucilla turns to me, looking very worried[4].

"An accident!" I shriek hysterically[5]. "What kind of an accident?"

"How should I know? It was just an idea!"

"Yeah, a really stupid idea!"

"Then tell me what you talked about when you met for the last … two days ago."

"Are you going to take the accident theory back?"

"Yes."

"Good," I sigh[6]. "It was great fun, as always. We were at the swimming pool, and Sven caught[7] me a sausage[8]."

"He did what?"

"It was a joke. He had a stick and some string[9] with him, and a fried sausage was dangling[10] on the end of it. He said it was really fresh, because he'd just fished it out of the pool."

· · · · · · · · ·

1 **to get in touch with sb.** – *jdn. kontaktieren, sich bei jdm. melden*
2 **to give sb. a grateful hug** – *jdn. dankend umarmen*
3 **I keep walking along beside Lucilla** – *ich laufe weiter neben Lucilla her*
4 **looking very worried** – *besorgt dreinschauend*
5 **to shriek hysterically** – *hysterisch schreien*
6 **to sigh** – *seufzen*
7 **to catch** – hier: *fangen*
8 **sausage** – *Wurst*
9 **string** – *Schnur, Bindfaden*
10 **to dangle** – *baumeln*

11

Lucilla looks at me wide-eyed.

"You know what he's like[1]! I almost died of laughter[2]… So that can't have been the problem."

"Wasn't there anything else?" Lucilla keeps up[3] the questioning.

"No. Well, apart from the thing with the mayonnaise."

"What thing with the mayonnaise?"

I sigh. Do I really have to tell the story? It's a bit embarrassing[4].

I take a deep breath[5]. "My mum had been shopping, and I'd asked her to buy me some suntan lotion[6]. When she came back, I asked her if she'd bought the lotion, and she said it was in one of the two shopping bags she'd just brought in. She held out a bag to me, so full that it was bursting at the seams[7], and I grabbed what I thought was the suntan lotion[8]."

"But it wasn't?"

"No, it was mayonnaise. But I only realised[9] that when I started rubbing it into Sven's back. It didn't soak into the skin at all[10]. Then Sven took the tube out of my hand and made some comment about how I should know by now that he prefers ketchup[11]."

"Well, there you go, it's pretty obvious[12]. That's why he dumped you." Lucilla nods, her mind now at rest[13].

"That wasn't it," I say.

• • • • • • • • •

1 **you know what he's like** – *du kennst ihn ja*
2 **I almost died of laughter** – *ich bin fast gestorben vor Lachen*
3 **to keep sth. up** – *mit etw. nicht aufhören*
4 **embarrassing** – *peinlich*
5 **to take a deep breath** – *tief Luft holen*
6 **suntan lotion** – *Sonnenmilch*
7 **it was bursting at the seams** – hier: *sie platzte aus allen Nähten*
8 **I grabbed what I thought was the suntan lotion** – *Ich griff nach dem, was ich für die Sonnenmilch hielt*
9 **to realise** – *merken*
10 **it didn't soak into the skin at all** – *sie zog überhaupt nicht in die Haut ein*
11 **to prefer ketchup** – *lieber Ketchup mögen*
12 **pretty obvious** – *völlig klar*
13 **mind at rest** – *beruhigt*

"Wasn't he angry?"

"Come on, Lucilla, it was an accident! Sven laughed his head off[1] and just said that it was typical of me. Only I could do something as stupid as that. The only really bad thing was that we both got sunburnt[2], but there are creams for that."

"Oh well, maybe he's just waiting for the sunburn to go before he calls you."

"But that was two days ago. Two valuable[3] days of holiday!" I grumble[4].

"Maybe there's a completely different explanation," suggests Lucilla.

"Oh, and what might that be then?" We're at the ice-cream parlour[5] now, and are about to[6] go in, when Lucilla grabs my arm and pulls me back.

"Oh my God, it's Sven!" she shouts.

"It can't be!" I peer cautiously[7] into the ice-cream parlour. "You're right! It's Sven sitting there! With two girls!"

Lucilla holds up her hand to her mouth, shocked. "No! Oh my God! That's probably why he hasn't called you."

"No," I say after a moment's thought. "Two girls are OK. It would be worse if it was one girl."

Lucilla nods. "True", she says, "unless he hasn't decided[8] yet."

"Decided what?"

"You know – which one. Maybe one of them is just a back-up[9] if

· · · · · · · · ·

1  **to laugh one's head off** (Redewendung) – *sich kaputtlachen*
2  **to get sunburnt** – *sich einen Sonnenbrand holen*
3  **valuable** – *wertvoll*
4  **to grumble** – *meckern, murren*
5  **ice-cream parlour** – *Eisdiele*
6  **to be about to do sth.** – *kurz davor sein, etw. zu tun*
7  **to peer cautiously** – *heimlich/zögernd spähen*
8  **to decide** – hier: *sich festlegen*
9  **back-up** – *Reserve*

the girl he chooses says no."

"What are you talking about?" I snap.

"About Sven's new girlfriend," replies Lucilla, as if it were[1] the most natural thing in the world.

I look at her furiously[2]. Then I turn around and run home.

My holidays are ruined. I might just as well have kept going to school[3] – even that couldn't possibly be any more depressing than what I'd just seen in that ice-cream parlour.

```
Love-Question 1
☑ INBOX
from: Lucilla Mobile


Ur not angry at me
about the accident-
thing, r u? :-( XXX
Lu
```

## Thursday 10ᵗʰ July

"Jojo, wake up! You can't just sleep through a whole precious[4] day of the holidays!" Someone is calling from the landing[5].

Sometimes my mum is in an unbearably good mood.[6] Besides, I don't want to sleep through the holidays; I want to sleep through the rest of my life!

"Aren't you going to get up?" she asks.

· · · · · · · · ·

1 **as if it were** – *als ob es wäre*
2 **furiously** – *wütend*
3 **I might just as well have kept going to school** – *Ich hätte genauso gut weiterhin zur Schule gehen können*
4 **precious** – *wertvoll*
5 **landing** – *(Treppen)flur*
6 **in an unbearably good mood** – *unerträglich gut gelaunt*

"No!" There, that's plenty of information. A simple answer to a simple question. But then Mum comes into the room; I withdraw[1] under my pillow[2].

"But Jojo," says Mum as she sits down next to me on the bed, "I expect you've got all sorts of plans with Sven. So, come on, rise and shine[3]!"

"I don't want to," I mumble from underneath the pillow.

"If I were you[4], I wouldn't leave Sven waiting too long. Who knows, he might start looking elsewhere[5]."

"Can't you go and bug[6] Flippi instead?" I'm shouting from under my pillow.

"Jojo, what's the matter with you[7]?" asks Mum, worriedly patting[8] the pillow.

"Nothing!" I sob[9]. "I just want to be left in peace!"

"Alright then." Mum stands up. "But if you want to talk about it ..." she adds.

"No!" No way. I know the routine: Mum makes tea and then we settle down to have a cosy little chat[10] and solve all my problems. Yeah, right![11] That's about the last thing I want right now. Mum leaves the room - at last. Can't anyone be left in peace to suffer[12] alone in this house?

· · · · · · · · ·

1 **to withdraw** - hier: *sich verkriechen*
2 **pillow** - *Kopfkissen*
3 **Rise and shine!** (Redewendung) - *Raus aus den Federn!*
4 **If I were you** - *an deiner Stelle*
5 **to look elsewhere** - *sich woanders umschauen, anderweitig schauen*
6 **to bug** (Umgangssprache) - *nerven*
7 **What's the matter with you?** - *Was ist mit dir los?*
8 **to pat** - *klopfen*
9 **to sob** - *schluchzen*
10 **a cosy little chat** - *ein Pläuschchen*
11 **Yeah, right!** - *Ja klar!* (ironisch)
12 **to suffer** - *leiden*

Soon afterwards, the door opens and my annoying little sister Flippi comes in and falls onto my bed. Great. Is there nowhere else in this house to sit down apart from[1] my bed?

"Now listen," says my sister, getting straight to the point[2], "I'm planning on creating a new breed of snail[3] - and you're going to help me. As an expert, so to speak," said Flippi sternly[4].

I peer out[5] from under my pillow. "Get out!" I yell[6] at her.

"Wait a second. You get the prototype, and you can even keep it. What do you think about a breed of snails for people in love[7]?" she asks, dying to[8] see my reaction.

I sob out loud. "Can't you all just leave me in peace[9]?" I shout and jump out of bed. I drag Flippi off the edge of my bed, push her out of my room, slam the door[10] and lean against it.

Flippi is so surprised that she even forgets to defend herself. It is only when she realises that she is outside the room that she grasps[11] what has just happened and starts hammering on the door. "You idiot! You've gone crazy! I wanted to give you a share of my profits[12], I might even have made you an equal partner. But you can forget it now. And you'd better lock the door[13]," she threatens.

Of course, that is the answer to all my problems! Lock the door!"
I was just about to!" I shout through the door and fumble[14] for the

. . . . . . . . .
1 **apart from** - *abgesehen von, außer*
2 **to get straight to the point** - *direkt zur Sache kommen*
3 **breed of snail** - *Schneckenzucht*
4 **stern** - *streng, unnachgiebig*
5 **to peer out** - *hier: spähen*
6 **to yell** - *schreien*
7 **in love** - *verliebt*
8 **to be dying to do sth.** - *es kaum erwarten können, etw. zu tun*
9 **to leave sb. in peace** - *jdn. in Frieden lassen*
10 **to slam the door** - *die Türe zuknallen*
11 **to grasp** - *begreifen*
12 **profits** - *Gewinn*
13 **you'd better lock the door** - *du solltest lieber die Türe abschließen*
14 **to fumble for sth.** - *nach etw. tasten*

key. Damn! Where is the key? I have to lock the door urgently[1]. Flippi doesn't mess around when it comes to acts of vengeance[2]. As I can't find the key, I have no other choice but[3] to drag[4] my desk over and put in front of the door. Just to make things crystal clear, I call out into the corridor: "And just so you all know, I'm never ever going to leave my room again. I'm going to stay here until I'm old and grey. So get used to it[5]! No one is ever going to come in through this door again." So, maybe now we can finally get some peace. Then I throw myself back into bed and pull the covers over my head.

All of a sudden someone knocks at my window. Oskar is standing on a ladder outside my window, waving at me. He has a cup of tea in his hand.
I open the window. "What is it?"
"Hello, Jojo, your mum said I should bring you a cup of tea." Oskar hands me the cup. "Can I come in?"
I think about it for a second. Since he is here, I might as well talk to him[6]. At the end of the day[7], Oskar is the most reasonable[8] member of our family – which probably has something to do with the fact that he isn't related to us. He's just Mum's boyfriend, my dad having legged it[9] when Flippi was still in nappies[10], and Oskar

· · · · · · · · ·
1 **urgently** – *dringend*
2 **Flippi doesn't mess around when it comes to acts of vengeance** – *Flippi ist nicht zimperlich, wenn es um Rache geht*
3 **I have no other choice but ...** – *mir bleibt nichts anderes übrig, als ...*
4 **to drag** – *schleifen, schleppen*
5 **So get used to it!** – *Dabei bleibt es und basta!*
6 **... I might as well talk to him** – *... kann ich auch mit ihm reden*
7 **at the end of the day** – *letztendlich, schließlich*
8 **reasonable** – *vernünftig*
9 **to leg it** (Umgangssprache) – hier: *abhauen*
10 **nappy** – *Windel*

has been part of our family for a while – for which he should be awarded a medal for bravery[1]. You see, I'm not all that difficult, but Flippi is a real public nuisance[2], and my mother – whoa – I can't even begin to describe how complicated she is. Maybe I should let him in. Oskar will probably be able to restore my confidence[3]. Then I'll feel better. "Come in," I growl[4]. Oskar clambers[5] in through the window and takes the cup of tea back out of my hand. Then he takes a look around my room and eventually sits down on the chair at my desk. I like that. At last, someone who doesn't immediately sit on my bed. I am a bit confused by the fact he's taken the tea away from me. Actually, I quite fancied[6] a cup of tea. Oskar takes a sip[7], I look at him in dismay[8]. Hey, that was my tea! "Did you come here just to drink tea?" I snap at him.

"No, I just thought I'd come by in case you wanted to talk to someone."

"I don't want to talk to anyone!" And in order to emphasise[9] this, I stalk[10] back to bed and slip under the covers.

Oskar nods. "OK, fine," he says and takes another sip of tea.

Now that's just going too far[11]; I'll force him to talk to me! I sit up. "Oskar, you're a boy … er, I mean … a man. Well, just imagine[12] you were in love with a girl, what would you do?"

Oskar seems to have real difficulty answering the question. "Well

• • • • • • • • •

1 **medal for bravery** - *Tapferkeitsmedaille*
2 **public nuisance** - *Nervensäge, Störenfried*
3 **restore sb.'s confidence** - *das Selbstbewusstsein von jdm. wiederherstellen*
4 **to growl** - *knurren*
5 **to clamber** - *klettern*
6 **to quite fancy sth.** - *ziemliche Lust auf etw. haben*
7 **to take a sip** - *einen kleinen Schluck nehmen*
8 **in dismay** - *bestürzt*
9 **to emphasise** - *betonen*
10 **to stalk** - hier: *marschieren, sich stürzen*
11 **Now that's just going too far!** – *Das geht jetzt aber zu weit!*
12 **just imagine** - *stell dir nur vor*

… yes … I'd tell her."

I wave at him dismissively. "Yeah, yeah, obviously, but what else would you do?"

Oskar pulls a helpless face[1] again. He had no idea where to begin. "Is this one of these trick questions[2]?" he asks cautiously[3].

"No."

"Hm. What would I do if I was in love? Oh, I know - I'd invite the lady to dinner."

I shake my head. "I don't mean that either."

"What do you mean then?"

"OK, what I really mean is: what *wouldn't* you do?"

That doesn't seem to help him either. "Jojo," he says, almost begging[4] me, "I think it would be a lot better if you just told me what this is about. Ask me a concrete question."

"OK. If you were in love with a girl, would there be any reason not to call her? Like, not call her, not visit her, nothing at all?"

Oskar laughs. "No, that would hardly be a sign[5] of my love."

I burst into tears. It is as clear as clear can be[6]: Sven doesn't love me anymore! I cry and cry and can't stop.

Oskar is worried. "Did I say something wrong, Jojo? I can think about it again, if you like."

"No, it's OK, but I'd like to be alone now."

Oskar nods, overcome with remorse[7], and for a moment he glanc-

· · · · · · · · ·

1 **to pull a face** – *ein Gesicht ziehen*
2 **trick question** – *Fangfrage*
3 **cautiously** – *vorsichtig*
4 **to beg** – *betteln*
5 **sign** – *Zeichen*
6 **as clear as clear can be** – hier: *so was von klar*
7 **overcome with remorse** – *völlig zerknirscht*

es[1] from my barricaded[2] door to the window. After letting out a sigh, he clambers out of the window, leaving the cup of tea behind. It is now empty. For a while, I have some peace and quiet. Until I hear someone murmuring[3] in the corridor.

"Oh, hello, Sven," I hear Flippi say from in front of my door, "Who are the flowers for?"

Sven? With flowers?

"No. No chance at all, Sven. Jojo doesn't want to see anybody. She won't even come out of her room."

What? Is she crazy? Sven with flowers? And she wants to send him away? I tear the desk away from my bedroom door in record time and rush out[4]. But instead of Sven, I stumble[5] into Flippi, Mum and Oskar, all waiting in front of my room.

"That's the way to do it," says Flippi haughtily[6], turning on her heels. Oskar only just about manages[7] to hold me back before I charge at[8] Flippi and try to strangle[9] her. "You're mean[10]! You're all so mean!" I shriek.

Flippi turns to Mum and Oskar: "I only said I'd get her out of her room. You're responsible[11] for the rest." Then she goes.

I shout at them all that I'm going to move[12] to Lucilla's; she'll let me suffer in peace. Then I go back into my room. I'm going to get

• • • • • • • • •

1 **to glance** - *kurz blicken*
2 **barricaded** - *verbarrikadiert*
3 **to murmur** - *murmeln, raunen*
4 **to rush out** - *hinausstürzen*
5 **to stumble into sb.** - hier: *in jdn. hineinstolpern*
6 **haughtily** - *hochnäsig*
7 **Oskar only just about manages ...** - *Oskar schafft es gerade noch ...*
8 **to charge at** - *auf jdn. losgehen*
9 **to strangle** - *erwürgen*
10 **mean** - *gemein*
11 **responsible** - *verantwortlich*
12 **to move** - hier: *umziehen*

dressed and walk past Mum and Oskar with my head held high[1], then leave the house without saying another word. Yes, that's what I'll do. As soon as I've found a black T-shirt, that is, because I will probably never wear bright colours ever, ever again.

```
Love-Question 2
☑ INBOX
from: Lucilla Mobile


Hey sweetie! ( How r
u feeling today? Did
u talk 2 ur mum? x
```

## Thursday evening 10th July

TR. 03

Unfortunately, I only have one black T-shirt and – Sod's Law[2] – it has "Don't worry, be happy" written on it. What a disaster! But I can't afford to be choosy[3]. On the way to Lucilla's, I get really worked up about[4] my family. For all their efforts to try and cheer me up[5], I haven't had any time to suffer! I'm going through the biggest drama of my life, and I'm not even allowed to step back and wallow[6] in it! Why can't I just be in a bad mood? In my opinion, teenagers have a fundamental right[7] to be in a bad mood. There must be some law or other[8] to prevent family members from forcing their relatives to be in a good mood. As I stamp[9] along in my bad mood, I go through the last time I saw Sven in my mind.

· · · · · · · · ·

1 **with one's head held high** (Redewendung) – *hoch erhobenen Hauptes*
2 **Sod's Law** (Redewendung) – *Murphy's Gesetz* (Diese Lebensweisheit, die auf den amerikanischen Ingenieur Edward Murphy zurückgeht besagt: „Alles was schiefgehen kann, wird auch schiefgehen")
3 **choosy** – *wählerisch*
4 **to get worked up about sb./sth.** – *sich über jdn./etw. aufregen*
5 **to cheer sb. up** – *jdn. aufmuntern*
6 **to wallow** – *schwelgen, suhlen*
7 **fundamental right** – *Grundrecht*
8 **some law or other** – *irgendein Gesetz*
9 **to stamp** – *stampfen*

21

Something must have happened[1] which has made him never want to talk to me again. Hm, there was the episode with the sausage, the mishap[2] with the mayonnaise, and we talked about being romantic – or something like that. Oh no! That could be it! I had complained about Sven being so unromantic. I'd told him our relationship would be absolutely perfect if he could just be a bit more romantic.

"Do you think it's unromantic if I catch a sausage for you?" Sven asked with a grin[3].

"You see, that's what I mean," I said. "That's not romantic; it's silly." Sven didn't seem too happy about that. "Then get me an instruction manual[4] on being romantic, and I'll put on a bit of romance for you. Do you want me to write you a poem or sing you a serenade under your balcony? Ignoring the fact[5] that you don't actually have a balcony, of course."

"If I have to tell you what to do, then it's not romantic anymore. You have to surprise me!" I explained to him, pretty annoyed. I probably should have ended the discussion at that point[6], but unfortunately, I didn't. I said something about being romantic was always proof of someone's love[7]. By way of reply[8] Sven mumbled "rubbish" and hardly talked to me anymore. That's it! I've scared him off with my stupid whinging[9] about romance.

· · · · · · · · ·

1 **sth. must have happened** – *irgendetwas muss geschehen sein*
2 **mishap** – *Missgeschick*
3 **grin** – *Grinsen*
4 **instruction manual** – *Gebrauchsanleitung*
5 **ignoring the fact that ...** – *mal davon abgesehen, dass ...*
6 **I probably should have ended the discussion at that point ...** – *Ich hätte die Diskussion an dieser Stelle beenden sollen ...*
7 **proof of love** – *Liebesbeweis*
8 **by way of reply** – *als Antwort*
9 **whinging** – *Gejammer, Nörgelei*

I turn into the street where Lucilla lives and see her coming towards me, waving[1] a piece of paper. Lucilla gives me a hug and brandishes[2] the piece of paper cheerfully[3]. "I've got everything under control. Come on, let's go through the list."

"Hey, wait a second. How did you know I was coming?"

"Your mum called me and told me. She told me to be nice to you and look after you[4]!"

"Oh my God, I hate her so much! Why does she have to do things like that?"

"Because she cares about you[5]," said Lucilla, not even taking a moment to think about it, and holding the piece of paper under my nose.

"What's that?"

Lucilla beams[6]: "A list of boys who come into consideration[7]."

"Into consideration as what?"

"You know, as Sven's successor[8]."

I start crying.

Lucilla falters[9]. "So you don't like the idea?"

"No!"

Lucilla shrugs her shoulders. "I just wanted to help you."

"If you want to help me, then call Sven and ask him what's going on."

Lucilla hesitates[10], starts to speak, hesitates again, and then says: "I

. . . . . . . . .

1 **to wave** – hier: *herumwedeln*
2 **to brandish** – *schwenken*
3 **cheerfully** – *fröhlich*
4 **to look after sb.** – *sich um jdn. kümmern*
5 **she cares about you.** – *sie hat dich lieb*
6 **to beam** – *strahlen*
7 **to come into consideration** – *in Frage kommen*
8 **successor** – *Nachfolger*
9 **to falter** – *stocken*
10 **to hesitate** – *zögern*

already did."

"And?" I ask, panic in my voice.

"He fobbed me off[1]. 'I haven't got the time. I'm busy,' he said."

"Why didn't you get him to[2] tell you what's going on?"

"I did, but he just said he didn't want to say anything, because I would probably go and tell you straight afterwards[3]."

I am now a complete bag of nerves[4]. "This looks like the first case ever of somebody dumping somebody else but wanting to keep it a secret from them[5]," I blubber[6].

Lucilla looks at me compassionately[7]. "It's really tough[8], Jojo. I feel so sorry for you."

I sniffle. Lucilla is desperately trying to think of something. "What about if you just pretended[9] you didn't know he'd dumped you?"

I look at her, thinking about her suggestion. "Do you think that could work?"

Lucilla shrugs her shoulders. "It's worth a try[10]."

We walk along side by side for a while in silence. Then Lucilla says: "Come on, give him a call!"

"No!"

"But you can't just accept the situation as it is! OK, maybe he really does want to dump you – but he's at least[11] got to tell you!"

. . . . . . . . .

1 **to fob sb. off** – *jdn. abwimmeln*
2 **to get sb. to do something** – *jdn. dazu bringen, etw. zu machen*
3 **straight afterwards** – *direkt im Anschluss*
4 **bag of nerves** – *Nervenbündel*
5 **to keep something a secret from somebody** – *etw. vor jdm. geheim halten*
6 **to blubber** – *heulen*
7 **compassionately** – *mitfühlend*
8 **tough** – hier: *hart*
9 **to pretend** – *so tun als ob*
10 **it's worth a try** – *es ist einen Versuch wert*
11 **at least** – *zumindest*

Lucilla has a good point there[1].

All of a sudden, I feel my fighting spirit[2] returning. I won't just let Sven go without a struggle. Oh no, I'll fight for him[3]! Or if not me, Lucilla will fight for him.

"I've got it! You can follow Sven!" I shout with newfound courage[4].

"I don't know …" Lucilla doesn't seem too keen on[5] the idea.

"Yes, you do. Just shadow[6] him and let me know what he's up to every hour on the hour[7]!"

"Alright then, but only if you come with me."

"But that's the point: I don't want him to see me. He knows me."

"So? He knows me, too!"

"Alright then, forget that plan. Have you got another idea?"

Lucilla thinks for a moment. "Yes. You start making a mental list[8] of why it's better not to be together with Sven anymore," she suggests.

"What for?"

"You know, just in case it really is over. Then you might even be happy about it."

I look at Lucilla, dumbfounded[9]. There's no way I could ever, ever be happy about that.

. . . . . . . . .

1 **Lucilla has a good point there** – *Da ist was dran an dem, was Lucilla gerade gesagt hat*
2 **fighting spirit** – *Kampfgeist*
3 **to fight for sb.** – *um jdn. kämpfen*
4 **newfound courage** – *neu entdeckter Mut*
5 **keen on sth.** – *begeistert von etw.*
6 **to shadow** – *beschatten, verfolgen*
7 **every hour on the hour** – *jede volle Stunde*
8 **to make a mental list** – *eine Liste im Kopf machen*
9 **dumbfounded** – *sprachlos*

"It's just a safety precaution[1]," Lucilla tries to soften[2] her words. "Come on, let's go for a walk in the park, and you can think about it."

I don't want to go for a walk. I ask Lucilla if it wouldn't be a better idea to make ourselves comfortable on a bench in the sun. I can think better sitting down.

"Alright then, but I hope you've got some mayonnaise with you," giggles[3] Lucilla. "The sun is red-hot[4] and I don't want to get sun-burnt!"

"Ha, ha! Really funny," I growl angrily. Then I try to concentrate. I look into the distance and think about what might be good about getting dumped by Sven. Three hours later, I still don't have a single argument. There just isn't one. Oh my God, what a nightmare[5]!

```
Love-Question 3
☒ INBOX
from: Lucilla Mobile

Hey honey! Have u
called Sven yet? ;-)
Txt back! Xxx
```

## Friday 11th July

TR. 04

After Lucilla and I spent yesterday looking at my situation from every possible angle[6], we decided it was a hopeless case and that I'd be better off[7] spending a few days practising the honourable art of

. . . . . . . . .

1 **safety precaution** – *Sicherheitsmaßnahme*
2 **to soften** – *abmildern*
3 **to giggle** – *kichern*
4 **red-hot** – *glühend heiß*
5 **nightmare** – *Albtraum*
6 **from every possible angle** – *aus jedem erdenklichen Blickwinkel*
7 **I'd be better off** – *ich sollte lieber*

suffering[1]. At home. In my room – which I will never leave again until I'm an adult. Or at least until the holidays are over. Meanwhile Lucilla will take care of shadowing Sven.

As it happens[2], I've only just settled down[3] in bed when Lucilla calls to give her first report. She's followed Sven to the supermarket, then a flower shop, a bookshop (he was in the cookery section[4]), and – this is the worst bit[5]! – has seen him in the ice-cream parlour with the same two girls as before, deep in conversation[6]. I've had enough; Sven owes[7] me an answer – now! I tell Lucilla to corner[8] Sven and get him to tell her what's going on. But Lucilla has this crazy idea that I should do it myself! I really don't know what's going on in her head sometimes. Talk about stupid[9]! After all, we've both decided that I should never leave my room ever again: and it's difficult to deal with stuff[10] when you're stuck[11] in a room of four by six metres. I tell Lucilla that I'll have to think again about[12] the whole "spending the rest of my life in my room" thing.

"Good idea," she says. "It's boiling hot today, so I'm going to the pool[13] now. Let me know what you decide."

"How am I meant to do that[14] if you're at the pool?" I grumble, annoyed that my best friend will be hanging out[15] at the pool while I

· · · · · · · · · ·

1 **the honourable art of suffering** – hier: *die hohe Kunst des Leidens*
2 **as it happens** – *wie der Zufall das so will*
3 **to settle down** – hier: *es sich bequem machen*
4 **cookery section** – *Kochbuchabteilung*
5 **this is the worst bit** – *jetzt kommt das Schlimmste*
6 **deep in conversation** – *tief im Gespräch versunken*
7 **to owe sb. something** – *jdm. etw. schuldig sein*
8 **to corner sb.** – *jdn. stellen*
9 **Talk about stupid!** – *Wie dumm kann man bitte sein?*
10 **to deal with stuff** – *sich um Dinge kümmern*
11 **to be stuck** – *festsitzen*
12 **to think again about something** – *sich etw. nochmal überlegen*
13 **pool** – hier: *Freibad*
14 **to be meant to do sth.** – *etw. tun sollen*
15 **to hang out** – *abhängen*

have to stay here in my room.

"I'll give you a call tonight."

"And what if I decide earlier?"

"Then just come down to the pool."

"Never!"

"Alright then," she says, "I'll just give you a call every two hours and you tell me how it's going. OK?"

Why is everything always so simple for Lucilla?

My life is one big disaster[1]. I realise this as Flippi appears in my room all of a sudden[2]. "Have you ever thought about knocking?" I snap at her.

"Waste of time," is all Flippi has to say to that. Then she pushes a box over to me. "Here, that's for you. It's a new breed. A lovesick[3] snail. It's bound to[4] help."

"A lovesick snail?"

"Yeah, she can keep you company[5] while you sit in your room. And she'll always be there to listen to you. But don't overdo it[6]! She might need a break at some point, too."

I'm touched[7]. "That's really ni…" I just manage to stop myself[8]. If there's one thing that Flippi can't stand[9], it's being called nice or sweet. She gives me a look of warning. I pat her on the shoulder. "You know what I mean … Thanks."

· · · · · · · · · ·

1 **one big disaster** – *eine einzige Katastrophe*
2 **all of a sudden** – *auf einmal*
3 **lovesick** – *liebeskrank*
4 **it's bound to help** – *es wird dir auf jeden Fall helfen*
5 **to keep sb. company** – *jdm. Gesellschaft leisten*
6 **Don't overdo it!** – *Übertreib's nicht!*
7 **touched** – *gerührt*
8 **I just manage to stop myself.** – *Ich bekomme es gerade noch hin, mich wieder einzukriegen.*
9 **to not be able to stand sth.** – *etw. nicht ertragen können*

"It's alright. Oskar gave me five euros for it," she explains.

Just like that[1], I'm no longer touched by this gesture[2].

"But now you have to take her for a walk[3]. She needs fresh air and exercise," says Flippi.

"What? I thought she was meant to keep me company."

"Yes, but she also needs a change of air occasionally[4]. The best place for her is the swimming pool…"

I look at Flippi suspiciously[5]. "Oskar has offered you extra cash if you get me to leave my room, right?"

Flippi nods.

"Forget it," I bark[6] at her, pointing to the door.

Flippi walks out of my room, leaving me behind with the snail in a box.

I open the box and look at the snail.

"Hello, I'm Jojo," I introduce myself[7]. "And I've got problems with my boyfriend, but you'll probably be hearing a lot more about that." Hey, just a moment[8]! Why am I pouring out my heart[9] to some snail? Oh my God! I've gone mad. And it's all Sven's fault. And why hasn't Lucilla given me a call? Then the phone rings! At last, at last, at last! Wait! Stop! Don't answer the phone! It wouldn't do any harm to Lucilla if she was left to worry about me[10] for a bit. Leaving me here all on my own like that. I open the door and call

. . . . . . . . .

1 **just like that** – *auf einmal, schlagartig*
2 **gesture** – *Geste*
3 **walk** – hier: *Gassi*
4 **occasionally** – *hin und wieder*
5 **suspiciously** – *misstrauisch*
6 **to bark** – *bellen*
7 **to introduce oneself** – *sich vorstellen*
8 **just a moment** – *moment mal!*
9 **to pour out one's heart to somebody** – *jdm. seine ganze Leidensgeschichte erzählen*
10 **to worry about sb.** – *sich um jdn. Sorgen machen*

out into the corridor. "I'm not here, whoever it is[1]. OK?"

"OK," say all three of them together.

Ha! That will teach Lucilla[2]. But then my curiosity gets the better of[3] me, and five minutes later I poke my head around the door[4].

"So? What did Lucilla want?"

"It wasn't Lucilla," replies Flippi.

I slam my bedroom door shut again. Well, great. She's already forgotten about me. She's having fun at the pool the whole time while I'm just sitting here and …

My door opens. Flippi looks in and says, "You're supposed to go to the park tomorrow afternoon at five o'clock."

"Lucilla can forget it!" I shout. "She can go for a walk in the park on her own."

"Or she can meet up with Sven. He called and wanted to speak to you. He wants to meet you tomorrow in the park."

"Sven!!!" I shriek hysterically. "Sven! Why didn't anyone let me know it was him? Why didn't someone tell me to come to the phone?"

Flippi rolls her eyes[5] and calls into the corridor, "Mum, I think it's finally happened: she's cracked[6]. That's it. Do we really have to keep her here? I mean, there are some really great homes[7]."

"Flippi, be quiet!" Mum appears in the doorway, shoves[8] Flippi back into the corridor and smiles at me warmly. "See? There you

• • • • • • • • •

1 **whoever it is** - *wer auch immer es sein mag*
2 **That will teach Lucilla!** - *Das geschieht Lucilla auch recht!*
3 **to get the better of sb.** - *die Oberhand über jdn. gewinnen*
4 **I poke my head around the door** - *ich schaue kurz zur Türe hinaus*
5 **to roll one's eyes** - *die Augen verdrehen*
6 **to crack** (Umgangssprache) - *durchdrehen*
7 **home** - hier: *psychiatrische Anstalt*
8 **to shove** - *schubsen*

are. Everything's going to be fine. I'd already guessed[1] something was up with Sven[2]…"

"Just leave me alone[3]!" I cut Mum short[4] with my whingey[5] voice. "OK, OK," she says, nodding her head. "If you want a chat or a cup of tea … you know … anytime!"

She carefully closes the door behind her, and her pity[6] only makes me more angry. But I don't have time to dwell on[7] my mum. First, I have to deal with Sven's call. Unfortunately, I can't get enthusiastic about it[8]. I still have a lump in my throat[9]. And probably rightly so. Sven has asked me to come to the park tomorrow afternoon. Is that a good sign? If everything is like it was before, then he would have just come over and asked me. He wouldn't have called and left a message[10]. Which means: no, this is not a good sign. I swallow[11]. He wants to dump me in public. He probably just wants to avoid a scene and thinks it will be too embarrassing for me to cry or have a go at him[12] in public. Well, he's wrong there! On the other hand … maybe I should play it really cool, as if I couldn't care less. That's it! I'll listen to whatever he has to say without batting an eyelid[13]. Or I can dump him myself. As soon as I see him, I'll smile coolly and tell him that, unfortunately, I don't have time for him anymore and that it would be better if we called

· · · · · · · · ·

1 **to guess** - *raten, ahnen*
2 **something was up with Sven** – *irgendetwas war mit Sven*
3 **Leave me alone!** – *Lass mich in Ruhe!*
4 **to cut sb. short** – *jdm. das Wort abschneiden*
5 **whingey** - *weinerlich*
6 **pity** – *Mitleid*
7 **to dwell on sb./sth.** – *lange über jdn./etw. nachdenken*
8 **to get enthusiastic about sth.** - *sich für etw. begeistern*
9 **to have a lump in one's throat** - *einen Kloß im Hals haben*
10 **to leave a message** - *etw. ausrichten lassen, eine Nachricht hinterlassen*
11 **to swallow** - *schlucken*
12 **to have a go at sb.** (Umgangssprache) - *jdn. anschnauzen*
13 **without batting an eyelid** - *ohne mit der Wimper zu zucken*

it a day[1]. Then I'll turn around and leave. Then I can bawl my eyes out[2] at home. Exactly. That is clearly the best idea. After settling on this plan, I cry a bit. Well, not exactly a bit: I absolutely bawl my eyes out.

```
Love-Question 4
☑ INBOX
from: Lucilla Mobile

Hey! R u alright?
Come 2 the pool! Did
Sven call yet? x
```

## Saturday 12ᵗʰ July

TR. 05

Lucilla calls – at last – and tells me that I really should end my self-inflicted[3] incarceration[4]. The weather is just too good and there is so much going on at the pool, and the summer holidays have only just begun. And anyway, I should put things with Sven behind me[5] and get on with my life[6]. When I tell her that I'm going to meet Sven in the park, she says that – strictly speaking – it would be great if he dumped me there. After all, I'm still so young, and there are so many other nice boys around[7]. Normally, I would disagree with her[8], of course, because Sven is by far[9] the nicest boy I've ever met. But under the current circumstances[10], I'm not feeling quite as positive about him as usual. The plan is to make a really cool exit in the park so that Sven feels sorry

· · · · · · · · ·

1 **to call it a day** – *einen Schlussstrich ziehen*
2 **to bawl one's eyes out** – *sich die Augen ausheulen*
3 **self-inflicted** – *selbst auferlegt*
4 **incarceration** – *Einkerkerung*
5 **to put sth. behind oneself** – *über etw. hinwegkommen*
6 **to get on with one's life** – *sein Leben wieder in die Hand nehmen*
7 **there are so many other nice boys around** – *es gibt so viele andere nette Jungs*
8 **to disagree with sb.** – *jdm. widersprechen*
9 **by far** – *bei Weitem*
10 **under the current circumstances** – *unter den jetzigen Umständen*

about ever even having thought about dumping me. We have a step-by-step [1] plan of how I'm going to do it. I will get to the park fifteen minutes late, just to make him wait. Then I won't even let him get a word out [2]; I'll just say - in my sweetest, most sugary [3] voice, "Hi, Sven, so nice of you to wait. And while we're on the subject of [4] waiting, I just wanted to let you know: you needn't wait for me anymore in the future, because I won't have time for you. But don't take it too hard [5], you're bound to find another nice girl [6]." Then, I'll turn around and strut [7] off in the best of moods. It's a good plan.

Of course, the fact that I end up [8] arriving fifteen minutes early, and have to wait impatiently for Sven in front of the park, means that the plan doesn't get off to a good start [9]. Sven comes up to me with a big smile on his face. Isn't that great?! He is actually [10] happy to be getting rid of me. He even has a rose in his hand. I see, now that it's all over he starts putting on [11] the romance. As he goes to kiss me, I turn my face to the side.

"Nice of you to wait," I start my planned speech.

"What do you mean?" asks Sven.

Oh no! What a mess! [12] Of course that doesn't make sense anymore.

· · · · · · · · ·

1 **step-by-step** – *Schritt für Schritt*
2 **to let sb. get a word out** – *jdn. zu Wort kommen lassen*
3 **sugary** – *zuckersüß*
4 **and while we're on the subject of waiting** – *und wo wir beim Thema Warten sind*
5 **to take sth. hard** – *etw. schwernehmen*
6 **you're bound to find another nice girl** – *du wirst bestimmt ein anderes nettes Mädchen kennenlernen*
7 **to strut** – *stolzieren*
8 **the fact that I end up ...** – *die Tatsache, dass ich letztendlich ...*
9 **to get off to a good start** – *einen guten Start hinlegen*
10 **actually** – *wirklich, tatsächlich*
11 **to put on sth.** – *mit etw. um die Ecke kommen*
12 **mess** – *Murks, Schlamassel*

Looks like[1] I'll have to improvise. "You wanted to talk to me?" I ask, coolly.

Sven grins. "Not so much talk to you; I wanted to show you something. Come with me."

I hold up my wrist[2] and look at my watch, trying to seem bored[3]. "I haven't got much time." Sven points at my wrist. "Yeah, and you haven't got a watch on either."

I look again at my wrist. Damn it, Sven is right. "I always tell the time by looking at my wrist. There's a trick I know." Just don't show any weakness[4]. So far, so good[5].

"Here," says Sven, handing me the rose. Then he points to the grass. "You just have to follow the roses."

I am amazed[6] by what I see: there are roses lying in the grass in a line. They stretch[7] over the lawn like a path, going past a big fat tree and into a hedgerow[8]. OK. He's obviously come up with a very extravagant[9] way of dumping me. I sigh. Sven is such a sweetie[10]. It's such a shame. Now I just want to get it over and done with[11] as quickly as possible. As I walk along the path of roses, I confront him with it[12]: "Somebody I know saw you hanging out with two girls recently." It won't do him any harm to know that there is nothing he can keep secret from me. Will he deny[13] it?

· · · · · · · · ·

1 **looks like** - *sieht so aus, als ob*
2 **wrist** - *Handgelenk*
3 **bored** - *gelangweilt*
4 **weakness** - *Schwäche*
5 **so far, so good** - *so weit, so gut*
6 **amazed** - *erstaunt*
7 **to stretch** - *hier: sich erstrecken*
8 **hedgerow** - *Hecke*
9 **extravagant** - *extravagant, übertrieben*
10 **such a sweetie** - *sooo süß*
11 **to get it over and done with** - *etw. hinter sich bringen*
12 **to confront sb. with sth.** - *jdn. etw. vorhalten*
13 **to deny** - *verleugnen, zurückweisen,*

Sven nods. "Yeah, I needed a few tips."

I hold my breath¹. It's unbelievable²! He doesn't even have the decency to try³ and talk his way out of it. Tips? Never heard that one before⁴! He's been getting tips on how to dump someone! How low will he sink⁵? "Good, then let's get it over and done with." I stomp along. "Hey, saying 'let's get it over and done with' isn't exactly putting me in a good mood!" grumbles Sven.

"Well, great, that makes two of us."

Sven stops in his tracks. "Hey, Jojo, is something the matter?"

I snort scornfully⁶. This guy really has a nerve⁷. "Everything's just fine," I call over my shoulder to him and trudge on⁸. The track of roses ends in a large hedge. I fight my way through its branches⁹ and am almost bowled over¹⁰ by what I see on the other side. Behind the hedge there's a table covered in a long, white tablecloth¹¹ and a silver candelabra¹² with five arms. There are rose petals¹³ scattered¹⁴ on the table. It has been laid¹⁵ for two people, classy¹⁶, with expensive porcelain, proper serviettes and all. Meanwhile Sven has also crawled¹⁷ through the hedge and is standing next to me. He looks at me slightly irritably.

· · · · · · · · ·

1 **to hold one's breath** – *den Atem anhalten*
2 **unbelievable** – *unglaublich*
3 **he doesn't even have the decency to try** ... – *er versucht auch nicht einmal, zu ...*
4 **Never heard that one before!** – *Ach, wie originell!*
5 **How low will he sink?** – *Wie tief kann man sinken?*
6 **scornfully** – *verächtlich*
7 **this guy really has a nerve** – *der Typ hat vielleicht Nerven*
8 **to trudge on** – *trotten*
9 **branches** – *Geäst*
10 **bowled over** – *sprachlos*
11 **tablecloth** – *Tischdecke*
12 **candelabra** – *Kronleuchter*
13 **rose petals** – *Rosenblüten*
14 **to scatter** – *streuen*
15 **laid** – *gedeckt*
16 **classy** – *vornehm, edel*
17 **to crawl** – *krabbeln*

"For you," he says gruffly¹, pointing at the table.

I gulp². "Well, marvellous," I say, furious. "Why didn't you ever do something like this when we were still together?"

"What do you mean?" asks Sven.

I have tears in my eyes. "It's sooo romantic!" I sob.

Sven grabs me by the arm and pulls me close to him. "Something's not right here," he says, looking me in the eyes. "Would you mind³ telling me what you're talking about?"

It can't go on like this⁴! I can't be bothered with⁵ Sven's fun and games anymore. Now I'm going to tell him to his face⁶ what is wrong. "You didn't call for five days," I start. "And you were having a great time with those other girls. And I know it's sometimes hard work being with me – well, at least that's what my mum says – but there's only one thing I really have to know: do you just need a break or is it over⁷?" I have to swallow audibly⁸ while talking, but I'm really proud of myself that I don't start to cry.

Sven puts his hand on my shoulder and looks me in the eyes. "Hey, you're not crying, are you?"

"No, I've got an allergy⁹ – and I've got something in my eye. Don't get it into your head that¹⁰ I'm crying about you. I don't care if you dump me!"

Sven looks at me, completely dumbfounded. Then he starts to

· · · · · · · · ·

1 **gruffly** – *schroff*
2 **to gulp** – hier: *schlucken*
3 **Would you mind ...?** – *Kannst du mir bitte ...?*
4 **It can't go on like this!** – *So geht das nicht weiter!*
5 **I can't be bothered with ...** (Umgangssprache) – *ich habe keine Lust auf ...*
6 **to tell sb. sth. to his face** – *jdm. etw. ins Gesicht sagen*
7 **to be over** – *vorbei sein*
8 **audibly** – *hörbar*
9 **to have an allergy** – *allergisch sein*
10 **Don't get it into your head that ...** – *Denk bloß nicht, dass ...*

laugh. "I don't believe it!" he snorts[1]. "That's typical Jojo again!"

I keep quiet, still feeling hurt. Sven stops laughing and takes me in his arms. "You complained[2] that I wasn't romantic enough, so I've really made an effort to put on some romance for you. I went and asked some girls from my class who know about this stuff, and they gave me this idea. I myself think it's all a bit silly really[3], but my team of experts said you'd be guaranteed to melt[4] in my arms when you saw it."

I look at him in disbelief[5]. "Does that mean it's not over?"

"Of course not! The things you get into your head, honestly ...[6]!"

"Well, I never…"

Sven kisses me, quickly, before I can say anything else.

Oh my God, I'm so happy! And then we sit down at the beautiful table. "Did you bring something to eat as well?" I ask.

"What do you think? I made it all myself. It was a lot of work." Sven bends down[7] under the table, and then jumps[8] straight back up in shock. He looks left and right in panic, runs through the hedge and back, looks at the table again, then underneath it, then into his empty hands and – in the end – he groans[9]: "Damn it! I left the food at home! Or it might still be in the car. My dad drove me here with all the stuff and I must have left the basket of food somewhere! I can't believe it!"

I giggle. Sven is still looking quite annoyed, but I can't be anything

· · · · · · · · ·

1 **to snort** – hier: *prusten*
2 **to complain** – *klagen, meckern*
3 **I myself think its a bit silly really** – *ich persönlich halte es für etwas doof*
4 **to melt** – *(dahin)schmelzen*
5 **in disbelief** – *fassungslos*
6 **honestly** – *also wirklich*
7 **to bend down** – *sich bücken*
8 **to jump** – *springen*
9 **to groan** – *ächzen*

except happy[1]. Sven and I are still together; I don't care about anything else[2]. And from now on, being romantic won't matter to me either. Although *this* is absolutely mega-romantic – I could get used to it. "So what are we going to do now?" I ask, laughing. Sven shrugs his shoulders. "Well, I'll go and get two portions of chips[3], and then we can eat them instead."

"I looove chips!"

Sven smiles and is in a better mood already. "I've got something else for you," he says. "You're not really meant to get it until dessert, but since our three-course menu has been, er, cancelled … Here…" Sven reaches into his trouser pocket[4] and pulls out a stack[5] of photos. Each photo shows Sven holding up a large letter[6] into the air. I look at him, curious[7].

Sven grins. "You just have to put the photos in the right order[8], and then you'll get a message!"

Hey, now that's exciting! I get straight to it. At first, it seems easy. "Yeliou," I shout! "But I've still got an 'o' and a 'v' left over[9]." Then I look at Sven. "What's that supposed to mean?"

Sven rolls his eyes. "It means you haven't got the letters in the right order."

Oh, right. Then I'll try again. It's much harder than I first thought. Iouley? Now I've got an 'o' and a 'v' left over. Wrong again. Ieoul? This time, there's a 'y' left over, along with the 'o' and the 'v'.

· · · · · · · · · ·

1 **I can't be anything except happy** – *ich bin nur noch glücklich*
2 **I don't care about anything else.** – *Alles andere ist mir egal.*
3 **chips** – *Pommes frites*
4 **trouser pocket** – *Hosentasche*
5 **stack** – *Stapel*
6 **large letter** – *Großbuchstabe*
7 **curious** - *neugierig*
8 **the right order** - *die richtige Reihenfolge*
9 **left over** - *übrig*

Sven sighs, gets up and helps me. He spreads the photos out[1] on the table in the right order. Oh, right, now it makes sense.
Smiling from ear to ear[2], I read the message out loud: "I love you!"
Sven grins. "I guessed that already, but it's nice to hear you say it."

"Oh, Sven! You're being unromantic again!" And I am a bit angry. But only a teeny-weeny[3] bit, of course. No, actually, I am not angry at all.

```
Love-Question 5
☑ INBOX
from: Lucilla Mobile


Hi babe! How did it
go with Sven? Tell me
what happened!! :-0
Lu Xxx
```

. . . . . . . . .

1 **to spread out** – *ausbreiten*
2 **to smile from ear to ear** – *über das ganze Gesicht lächeln*
3 **teeny-weeny** (Umgangssprache) – *klitzeklein*

# Hortense Ullrich

# The Football
# Pitch of Dreams

"I think they're in love," squeaks[1] Lucilla and gives me a nudge[2]. Great! Now the rest of my hotdog is no longer in the bread roll, but on the lap[3] of the person next to me. She hasn't noticed[4], however, and I'm not going to tell her either. If necessary, I'll deny that I ever had a hotdog. Anyway, it was a stupid idea that I should go and get hotdogs and popcorn – that's a recipe for disaster[5]. And of course I immediately got into trouble[6] at the hotdog stand. Because of my clumsiness[7] I am now forbidden to go anywhere near it[8].

"Who's in love with who? And how do you know?" I ask, looking longingly[9] at my hotdog as it sits on my neighbour's lap.

"He just looked at her, she went red and then looked away. Then she looked at him, he went red and then looked away very quickly too." Lucilla nods intently[10] and calls it "an unmistake-able sign[11]".

It does sound like[12] a good analysis, but who is she talking about? We're at the football pitch[13] and have to watch a game. Four teams are competing against each other[14] in a tournament and

· · · · · · · · ·

1 **to squeak** – *quieken*
2 **to give sb. a nudge** – *jdn. anschubsen*
3 **lap** – *Schoß*
4 **to notice** – *merken*
5 **That's a recipe for disaster.** (Redewendung) – *Da ist die Katastrophe schon vorprogrammiert.*
6 **to get into trouble** – *Ärger bekommen, in Schwierigkeiten geraten*
7 **act of clumsiness** – *Ungeschicklichkeit*
8 **forbidden to go anywhere near it (the stand)** – *verboten, sich dem Stand künftig auch nur zu nähern*
9 **longingly** – *sehnsüchtig*
10 **intently** – *eifrig*
11 **unmistakeable** – *untrüglich*
12 **to sound like sth.** – *nach/wie etw. klingen*
13 **football pitch** – *Fußballplatz*
14 **to compete against each other** – *gegeneinander antreten*

our school team is playing; the two winners from before the lunch break are now playing for the local championship[1]. As this is all happening during the school day, we've been told to come whether football interests us or not. The result is that there are 200 pupils at the sports fields and Lucilla is able to check all of them for the first signs[2] of romance. She's good at it – I have no idea who she might mean[3], though. I look around and all I can see are other people from school. Some are busy eating[4] and the really keen ones[5] are doing homework. The rest are screaming and shouting[6] – seemingly[7] in no relation to[8] their team's performance.

"Who do you mean, then?" I ask after a pause.

"Well, Sara and our captain."

"Captain? We have a captain?"

"Jojo! Of course we have one. He is, like, the leader of the team – he speaks for them and organises them. And our captain is called Oliver, by the way.

"Oh, right[9]. Which Sara do you mean?"

"Bad-mood[10]-Sara."

· · · · · · · · ·

1 **local championship** - *Kreismeisterschaft*
2 **the first signs** - *die ersten Zeichen/Ansätze*
3 **to mean sb.** - *jdn. meinen, von jdm. sprechen*
4 **busy eating** - *mit Essen beschäftigt*
5 **the really keen ones** - *die ganz Eifrigen*
6 **to scream and shout** - *johlen und grölen*
7 **seemingly** - *allem Anschein nach*
8 **in no relation to** - *unabhängig von*
9 **oh, right** - *ach so, aha*
10 **bad mood** - *schlechte Laune*

"What? Never!" I snort[1], which gets me another nudge[2] from Lucilla. I fall quite hard against the person next to me, say sorry and manage to retrieve[3] the rest of my hotdog without her noticing[4]. I put it back into the bread roll and eat it as quickly as I can. Lucilla must have seen me because she looks at me in disgust[5].

"Jojo! What are you doing?! That's disgusting!"

"I was hungry!" I say in my defence[6].

"Then go get another hotdog! Whatever! But stop eating the ones that have fallen on the floor[7]."

If only it were that easy! I don't want to tell Lucilla anything about the whole not-being-allowed-near-the-hotdog-stand thing, so I change the subject – or rather[8], I return to the previous[9] subject.

"How can you fall in love[10] if you're always in a bad mood?"

"Even miserable[11] people can fall in love – why not, after all? And it can often mellow them out[12]!" says Lucilla in a lecturing[13] tone.

"Or they just get even more miserable when they realise that nobody wants to be with someone who is always in a bad mood!"

"You're too negative, Jojo."

· · · · · · · · ·

1 **to snort** – hier: *prusten*
2 **nudge** – *Schubs*
3 **to retrieve** – *borgen*
4 **without sb. noticing** – *unbemerkt*
5 **in disgust** – *angewidert*
6 **in my defence** – *zu meiner Verteidigung*
7 **the ones that have fallen on the floor** – *die Runtergefallenen*
8 **or rather** – *beziehungsweise*
9 **previous** – *vorhergehende*
10 **to fall in love** – *sich verlieben*
11 **miserable** – *übellaunig*
12 **to mellow sb. out** (umgangsprachlich) – *jdn. viel milder stimmen*
13 **lecturing** – *belehrend*

"Oh, am I? How come[1] I heard all the stories about Sara from you, then? And it was you who called her bad-mood-Sara anyway!

"Hmm," replies Lucilla.

I only know Sara from hearsay[2]. She goes to a different school, but Lucilla's mother is friends with Sara's and Lucilla has often been forced[3] by her mother to do stuff[4] with Sara. Lucilla is really annoyed[5] about this because, firstly, Sara is always in a bad mood and, secondly, she is a year younger than us and Lucilla doesn't like hanging around[6] with younger girls. After all, we've got enough trouble trying to be cool as it is[7]. I haven't really understood the rules yet; in fact, Lucilla says that my behaviour[8] is not exactly helping us to be accepted as cool[9]. There's nothing I can do about that, though. I always behave well[10], but sometimes life just seems to have it in for me[11] and so I always seem to end up in totally embarrassing[12] situations – situations that are so embarrassing that the only real solution is to just move to another

· · · · · · · · · ·

1 **How come I heard all the stories from you then?** – *Wieso habe ich dann die ganzen Geschichten von dir gehört?*
2 **hearsay** – *Hörensagen*
3 **to be forced** – hier: *verdonnert werden*
4 **to do stuff** – *etw. unternehmen*
5 **really annoyed about sth.** – *über etw. total sauer*
6 **to hang around with sb.** – *mit jdm. abhängen*
7 **as it is** – *schon, ohnehin*
8 **behaviour** – *Verhalten*
9 **to be accepted as cool** – *als cool gelten*
10 **to behave well** – *sich gut verhalten*
11 **to have it in for someone** – *es auf jdn. abgesehen haben*
12 **totally embarassing** – *oberpeinlich*

town. But my mum refuses[1] to move, and so I am very grateful to Lucilla that she's still my friend, even if she is actually often the reason why I end up looking stupid[2]. But hey, who cares?[3]

TR. 02 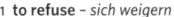 Sara has got Lucilla's interest[4] because Lucilla can smell romance[5]. And if there's one thing Lucilla loves, it's romance.

"Perhaps she didn't turn red because she's in love, but because she's red with anger that Oliver looked at her," I say, grinning[6] and taking a handful of popcorn from Lucilla's bag.

"Are you trying to rip[7] my bag or what?" asks Lucilla, annoyed. "And why didn't you buy your own popcorn if you're so hungry?"

I don't want to answer the last question because I did buy my own bag, but there was that little accident on the way over ... I need Lucilla to let me eat her popcorn and so I've got to keep her in a good mood. So I say: "Sorry Lucilla, you're probably right. It must be love."

"Of course I'm right! I know about love. I can see this kind of thing a mile off[8]!"

"Where is she?" I ask.

· · · · · · · · ·

1 **to refuse** – *sich weigern*
2 **to end up looking stupid** – *am Ende blöd dastehen*
3 **But hey, who cares?** – *Aber egal!*
4 **to get sb.'s interest** – *jdns. Interesse wecken*
5 **Lucilla can smell romance** – *Lucilla wittert Romantik*
6 **to grin** – *grinsen*
7 **to rip** – *reißen*
8 **I can see this kind of thing a mile off!** – *So was erkenne ich aus jeder Entfernung!*

Lucilla points to a girl dressed in black with the long dark hair and glasses. She is sitting right down in the front row[1] and is watching the game with a stony face[2].

"Wow, she looks in a bad enough mood from here! Where is he?"

"On the pitch, of course. He's playing."

"Which one is he then? They all look the same[3]."

"He's got the dark band around his upper arm; that's how you can tell he's captain[4]."

"And he's got time to look at Sara and go red while he's playing?"

"The ball was out of play[5]. He had the throw-in[6] and as he went to the edge[7] of the field, their eyes met. [8]"

Lucilla is amazing! She knows about football *and* is able to recognise a budding[9] romance from this far off[10].

"And do you think there was a spark between them[11]?"

"Yeah, I do. And I don't think they know each other yet, otherwise they wouldn't have gone red, but would have waved to each other or something like that[12]. So they'll need our help."

I look at Lucilla blankly[13].

· · · · · · · · ·

1 **first row** – *erste Reihe*
2 **stony face** – *versteinerte Miene*
3 **They all look the same.** – *Die sehen alle gleich aus.*
4 **That's how you can tell he's captain.** – *Daran erkennst du, dass er Kapitän ist.*
5 **out of play** – *aus*
6 **throw-in** – *Einwurf*
7 **edge** – hier: *Rand*
8 **Their eyes met.** – *Ihre Blicke haben sich gekreuzt*
9 **budding** – *knospend, beginnend*
10 **from this far off** – *aus dieser Entfernung*
11 **Was there a spark between them?** – *Hat es zwischen den beiden gefunkt?*
12 **or something like that** – *oder so*
13 **blankly** – hier: *verständnislos*

Lucilla makes a dramatic pause[1], and then says: "We're going to bring the two of them together."

I pull away from Lucilla: "Oh no! No no no! I don't want to have anything to do with it! It will be complete chaos."

"Of course it will be, unless you manage to keep yourself under control[2]. But since we've got to spend the entire day on the sports field and don't have anything else to do, let's play Cupid[3]!"

"What are you going to do?"

"We're going to turn them into a couple[4]!"

"But how?"

"I'll take care of Sara; after all, she's the daughter of a friend of my mum. You'll be responsible for Oliver[5]."

"But I don't know him at all[6]. All I know about him is his name, and you told me that."

"And? So what? That's enough – you can start by going up to him[7] and saying 'Hi, Oliver!'"

"Oh, great! And then follow it up with[8]: "By the way, bad-mood-Sara is crazy about you[9]!"?

"Well, I hope you think of something better than that!" says Lucilla angrily.

1 **a dramatic pause** – *ein Pause, um die Spannung zu erhöhen*
2 **to keep oneself under control** – *sich zusammenreißen*
3 **to play Cupid** – *Amor spielen*
4 **to turn them (two people) into a couple** – *zwei Menschen verkuppeln*
5 **to be responsible for** – hier: *übernehmen*
6 **But I don't know him at all.** – *Aber ich kenne ihn doch gar nicht.*
7 **to go up to someone** – *zu jdm. gehen*
8 **And then follow it up with...** – *Und gleich im Anschluss komme ich mit...*
9 **crazy about sb.** (Umgangssprache) – *verknallt in jdn.*

"Something like ... what? What's your plan?"

"After this game, we've got three hours until the final this afternoon. That'll be more than enough[1]. First off, I'm going to give Sara a makeover ..."

"You're going to do what?"

"You know, make her pretty. At the moment, she looks totally boring[2] und uncool – but give her another haircut[3] and a new outfit and she'll be a guaranteed hit!"

"In three hours?"

"I've got everything we need," says Lucilla, patting[4] her bag. And I believe her. After all, she restyles her look[5] several times a day.

"Appearance can really make the difference, you know," lectures Lucilla.

"I don't have to do the same with Oliver, do I?" I ask, frightened[6]. Lucilla looks horrified[7] and waves her hand[8].

"Are you mad? As if you could[9]! No, all you've got to do is to get Oliver to come[10] to the hotdog stand. I'll be waiting there with Sara and will take care of the rest."

. . . . . . . . .

1 **to be more than enough** – *dicke reichen*
2 **boring** – *langweilig, unscheinbar*
3 **haircut** – *Frisur*
4 **to pat** – *klopfen*
5 **to restyle one's look** – *sich umstylen*
6 **frightened** – *erschrocken*
7 **horrified** – *entsetzt*
8 **to wave one's hand** – *mit der Hand winken*
9 **As if you could!** – *Als ob du könntest!*
10 **to get sb. to do sth.** – *jdn. dazu bringen, etw. zu tun*

That actually sounds doable[1]. How hard can it be to lure[2] someone to a hotdog stand?

I nod. The game ends and our team has won; Lucilla hurries over[3] to Sara. I run after her[4]. When Lucilla gets to Sara, she hugs her and shouts happily, "Hey Sara, sweetie! I haven't seen you for ages![5]"

TR. 03 Sara tenses up[6] and looks at Lucilla, confused[7]: "But we went for a coffee with our mums last weekend:"

"Yes, but we didn't get a chance to have a chat[8]."

Sara takes a step back and replies cooly, "Well, that was because you ignored me and read your fashion magazines."

Lucilla doesn't let that stop her. She puts her arm around Sara and adds, as if nothing has been said[9], "Yes, and I got some great ideas. Did you know that I'm an expert at makeovers? I can turn a caterpillar into a butterfly!

"I don't buy that[10]. You're talking about a biological process and it doesn't need your help." Lucilla looks blankly[11].

. . . . . . . . .

1 **doable** – *machbar*
2 **to lure** – *locken*
3 **to hurry over to sb.** – *zu jdm. herübereilen*
4 **to run after someone** – *jdm. hinterherlaufen*
5 **I haven't seen you for ages** – *lange nicht mehr gesehen*
6 **to tense up** – *sich versteifen, sich anspannen*
7 **confused** – *verwundert*
8 **to have a chat** – *quatschen*
9 **As if nothing has been said.** – *Als hätte sie nichts gesagt.*
10 **I don't buy that.** – *Das glaub ich kaum; Das glaub ich dir nicht.*
11 **blankly** – hier: *verständnislos*

"When a caterpillar becomes a butterfly, it's called metamorphoses," lectures Sara. Lucilla knits her brow[1].

"What I wanted to say is this: I can turn a completely average[2] girl into an attractive catwalk[3] queen!" At this, Sara steps back and looks angrily[4] at Lucilla.

"What's that supposed to mean?"[5] Nice going, Lucilla![6]

"Well," says Lucilla, her face taking on something of a professional[7] expression, "Let us just suppose that[8] a girl likes a boy and wants him to notice[9] her, to talk to her and to, you know, invite her out for[10] pizza or a coke or to the cinema ..."

Lucilla observes that Sara shows a quiet interest. Lucilla is happy and continues talking.

" ... So this girl comes to me and asks me to help her. I give her a new look and, before you know it, she's reeling the guy in[11]."

"I don't believe you!" says Sara.

Lucilla points to me.

"Just ask Jojo!"

Sara appears to flinch[12].

· · · · · · · · ·

1 **to knit one's brow** – *die Stirn runzeln*
2 **completely average** – *völlig unscheinbar*
3 **catwalk** – *Laufsteg*
4 **angrily** – *verärgert, feindselig*
5 **What's that supposed to mean?** – *Was soll das denn heißen?*
6 **Nice going!** – ironisch: *Sehr geschickt!*
7 **professional** – *fachkundig, dienstlich, geschäftsmäßig*
8 **let us just suppose that...** – *nehmen wir mal an, dass...*
9 **to notice** – *merken*
10 **to invite sb. out for sth.** – *jdn. zu etw. einladen*
11 **to reel sb. in** (Umgangssprache) – *jdn. an der Angel haben*
12 **to flinch** – *zusammenzucken*

"What? Jojo the chaos queen?!" she asks.

I frown[1] and look angrily at Sara. Do I have this reputation for chaos even in other schools that I've never been to? And this girl Sara says it to my face[2]? What a great start! I'm supposed to help *her*[3]?! I try to get Lucilla to look at me[4] so that I can tell her without using spoken words that I am just not up for[5] this kind of thing. It's no use, Lucilla is already working out how to give Sara her makeover.

"How important are those glasses?" asks Lucilla.

"Very. I can't see anything without them." This answer doesn't seem to impress[6] Lucilla at all.

"Yes, but how bad is it without glasses? Can you at least recognise people?" she asks.

"Yes, but they're kind of blurry.[7]"

Lucilla waves her hand dismissively[8]. "That's fine. We can live with that."

"Well perhaps you can," contradicts[9] Sara, "but I need my glasses." Lucilla isn't phased[10] by this, though.

"Some guys don't like girls with glasses. We don't want to take the risk; so lose[11] the glasses."

· · · · · · · · ·

1 **to frown** - *die Augenbrauen zusammenziehen*
2 **to say it to someone's face** - *jdm. es ins Gesicht sagen*
3 **I'm supposed to help her?** - *Der soll ich helfen?*
4 **to get someone to do something** - *jdn. dazu bringen, etw. zu tun*
5 **to be up for sth.** - *Lust auf/zu etw. haben*
6 **to impress** - *beeindrucken*
7 **blurry** - *verschwommen*
8 **dismissively** - *wegwerfend*
9 **to contradict** - *widersprechen*
10 **phased** (Umgangssprache) - *aus dem Konzept gebracht*
11 **to lose** (Umgangssprache) - hier: *abziehen*

"I really don't know what you're talking about," says Sara and turns[1] to go.

"Do you know the captain of our football team?"

Sara stops, goes a little red[2] and replies stubbornly[3]. "No!"

"Jojo knows him," says Lucilla triumphantly[4]. Sara shrugs her shoulders[5], but stays where she is.

"That's nice for her," she says.

I pull Lucilla to me and hiss[6] quietly: "What are you saying? I don't know him!"

"Keep cool[7]. I know what I'm doing," whispers[8] Lucilla.

"Yeah, that'd be, like, the first time ever," I mumble[9] quietly. Lucilla turns back to Sara.

"You think he's cute[10], don't you? Jojo can help you two meet."

"How do you know I like him?" says Sara, hesitating[11]. Lucilla smiles slyly[12].

"You were cheering for the wrong team," she says.

. . . . . . . . .

1  **to turn** - *sich drehen*
2  **to go red** - *rot werden*
3  **stubbornly** - *trotzig, hartnäckig*
4  **triumphantly** - *triumphierend*
5  **to shrug one's shoulders** - *die Schultern zucken*
6  **to hiss** - *zischen*
7  **Keep cool!** - *Reg dich nicht auf!, Bleib cool!*
8  **to whisper** - *flüstern*
9  **to mumble** - *nuscheln, murmeln*
10 **You think he's cute.** - *Du findest ihn gut.*
11 **to hesitate** - *zögern*
12 **slyly** - *verschmitzt*

"Yeah, so what?[1] Perhaps I prefer[2] your team to ours?" replies Sara. This brings a smile to Lucilla's lips.

"But you only cheered when Oliver scored a goal."

"He's called Oliver?" says Sara, going red. Lucilla nods. Sara hesitates again; Lucilla moves closer to her and talks in an encouraging[3] way.

"Don't worry! Before this championship is over, you'll have conquered his heart[4]. And that's a promise!"[5]

Sara remains sceptical[6]. "Oh really? And I suppose I'll do this by letting you give me a makeover?"

"That's right. Now, first off[7], we'll have to get some colour into your wardrobe[8]," replies Lucilla and sets to work[9]. She takes two T-shirts out of her bag – Lucilla always has spare[10] T-shirts with her because, as she puts it[11], "You just never know when your mood might change and the T-shirt you put on in the morning doesn't suit anymore." Lucilla thinks it's important to be prepared[12] for this sort of thing. I've stopped complaining about it because Lucilla and her T-shirts have saved[13] me again and again when I've had ketchup, cola and pizza stains on mine.

· · · · · · · · ·

1 **So what?** (Umgangssprache) – *Na und?*
2 **to prefer sth.** – *etw. vorziehen*
3 **encouraging** – *aufmunternd*
4 **to conquer sb.'s heart** – *jdns. Herz erobern*
5 **That's a promise** – *Garantiert!*
6 **sceptical** – *skeptisch*
7 **first off** (Umgangssprache) – *als Erstes*
8 **wardrobe** – *Garderobe*
9 **to set to work** – *mit der Arbeit beginnen*
10 **spare** – *Wechsel-, Ersatz-*
11 **as she puts it** – *wie sie das sagt*
12 **prepared** – *vorbereitet*
13 **to save** – *retten*

She holds the two tops[1] next to Sara's face, leans her head to one side[2] and then decides. "We'll take the lime green[3]; you're more of a green person."

Sara still looks distrustful[4], but you can tell that her resistance[5] is crumbling[6]. Lucilla, meanwhile, takes out her make-up bag[7] and checks a couple of eye-shadow[8] and lipstick[9] colours by holding them up to Sara's face. "We've got everything we need," she says, satisfied[10].

Then she looks at Sara's haircut. "What about your hair?" she asks critically, "do you really like it long?"

Sara grabs at her hair, frightened[11], and shouts. "Yes I do!"

"Hmm. Then we'll have to layer it[12]."

"No!" shouts Sara.

"OK, but then we'll have to tie it back or, even better, tie it up at the very least[13]," says Lucilla strictly[14] and Sara nods, relieved[15].

. . . . . . . . .

1 **top** – hier: *Oberteil*
2 **to lean one's head to one side** – *den Kopf schief legen*
3 **lime green** – *lindgrün*
4 **distrustful** – *misstrauisch*
5 **resistance** – *Widerstand*
6 **to crumble** – *bröckeln*
7 **make-up bag** – *Schminkbeutel*
8 **eye-shadow** – *Lidschatten*
9 **lipstick** – *Lippenstift*
10 **satisfied** – *zufrieden*
11 **frightened** – *erschocken*
12 **to layer** – hier: *stufen*
13 **at the very least** - *wenigstens, zumindest*
14 **strictly** – *streng*
15 **relieved** – *erleichtert*

She even appears to be grateful[1] that she has been allowed to keep[2] her long hair. Lucilla really is good.

"Great!" says Lucilla, "then let's get started[3]. We're off to the changing rooms[4]". Lucilla sets off, Sara and me follow behind. Lucilla looks at me and nods in the vague[5] direction of the boys changing rooms. "Don't you have something to be taking care of[6]?"

I, however, don't want to 'take care' anything, because I know that Lucilla means that it's my job to go and find Oliver and lure him to the hotdog stand. Lucilla sees from the look on my face[7] that I don't want to go, so she pulls me aside[8] and whispers to me. "Come on, try and be romantic for once[9]. Hey, you might even learn something!" Oh no, now she's played the romance-card. I'm notoriously[10] bad about romance and Lucilla reckons[11] that, sooner or later, it'll catch up with me[12]. She says I should really start working on my romantic side. I look at her stubbornly. Lucilla starts to half-sing[13].

• • • • • • • • •

1 **grateful** – *dankbar*
2 **to keep** – *behalten*
3 **Let's get started!** – *Legen wir mal los!*
4 **changing rooms** – *Umkleide*
5 **vague** – *vage*
6 **Don't you have something to be taking care of?** – *Hast du nicht etwas zu erledigen?*
7 **to see sth. from the look on sb.'s face** – *etw. jdm. am Gesicht ansehen*
8 **to pull sb. aside** – *jdn. zur Seite ziehen*
9 **for once** – *nur ein Mal*
10 **notoriously** – *notorisch*
11 **to reckon** (Umgangssprache) – hier: *meinen, der Meinung sein*
12 **to catch up with sb.** – *jdn. einholen*
13 **half-sing** – *flöten*

"Young love! Young love! And you and me are making it happen! Now, off you go[1], Jojo, and do your bit[2]."

TR. 04    I sigh[3] and run off to the boys' changing rooms. As I grab the handle[4], I realise that I've got no business being there[5]. It's not only that I am completely uninterested in sport and for this reason alone[6] shouldn't be allowed on a sports field, it's also the fact that I am the wrong gender[7] for this changing room – after all, I'm not a boy. Hm. That could be a problem. So I let go of the handle and wait in front of the door, maybe I should call Oliver's name through the door?

I decide against that. There must be a way for me, for once, to do stuff in a completely normal way, nicely avoiding embarrassment[8]. So I decide to wait until Oliver himself comes out.

I wait in front of the door. I wait and wait. I walk back and forth. Then I lean on the wall next to the door. Then I get annoyed and slump down the wall[9] and sit on the floor.

It's only as the first group leaves the changing rooms that I realise that I won't be able to recognise[10] Oliver – unless he is wearing

· · · · · · · · ·

1 **Now, off you go!** – *Nun geh schon!*
2 **Do your bit.** – *Mach deinen Teil.*
3 **to sigh** – *seufzen*
4 **handle** – *Klinke*
5 **to have no business being there** – *dort nichts zu suchen haben*
6 **for this reason alone** – *allein aus diesem Grund*
7 **gender** – *Geschlecht*
8 **nicely avoiding embarrassment** – *schön ohne Peinlichkeit*
9 **to slump down the wall** – *die Wand hinunterrutschen*
10 **to recognise** – *erkennen*

a sign¹ saying "I am Oliver!" Quite honestly², they all look the same to me when they're playing – they all wear the same kit³, after all. The fact that they are all wearing tracksuits⁴ doesn't help, either, because Oliver's only distinguishing feature⁵ is the captain's armband. It would appear that he only wears this when playing, though. Now I have absolutely no chance of recognising him. Great. I mean, what does Lucilla expect me to do? Talk to every boy here and ask if he's called Oliver? Not on your life!⁶

"Hey you! You're not called Oliver by any chance⁷, are you?" I say to the next boy who comes out of the changing rooms. He and the boy next to him stop.
"Why?" he asks and looks at me curiously⁸. I'm not here to answer

```
Love-Question 1
☑ INBOX
from: Lucilla Mobile

Hey! Where r u? Have
u found Olli yet?
What r u w8ing 4?
```

questions, though, so I impatiently⁹ ask for a yes or a no.
"No," he replies.
So I turn to his friend. "What about you?"
"No. Why do you want Oliver?"

· · · · · · · · ·
1 **sign** – *Schild*
2 **quite honestly** – *ehrlich gesagt*
3 **kit** – *Spielkleidung, Trikot*
4 **tracksuit** – *Trainingsanzug*
5 **distinguishing feature** – *Unterscheidungsmerkmal*
6 **Not on your life!** – *Nie im Leben!*
7 **by any chance** – *zufällig*
8 **curiously** – *neugierig*
9 **impatiently** – *ungeduldig*

58

"Is he still in the changing rooms?" I continue, trying to avoid going into detail on that question[1]. Not out of impoliteness[2], of course, but because I don't have the slightest idea[3] what to reply.

"Yes, he is," replies the boy.

I stand up. "Oh, great. Can you get him out here?"

The boy puts his hands on his hips[4].

"What do you want?" he asks.

I pause for thought[5]. Now, I could say that the hotdog guy sent me because he wants to give Oliver a free[6] hotdog for scoring all those goals. Hm. But suddenly I jump[7] - hotdog stand?! Oh my God! I've forgotten that I'm not allowed anywhere near this hotdog stand. After I tried to carry my and Lucilla's hotdogs as well as two bags of popcorn I tipped[8] one entire[9] bag onto the grill. The guy on the stand went crazy, started swearing[10] and shouting and forbid me to ever come near him again. That's really annoying now.

Maybe I should just say that Sara likes him? No, I'd better not – in Lucilla's world that's an anti-romance-torpedo. Lucilla wants to play Cupid, and Cupid doesn't always say what he's planning

· · · · · · · · ·

1  **to go into detail on sth.** - *auf etw. eingehen*
2  **impoliteness** – *Unhöflichkeit*
3  **the slightest idea** - *die geringste Ahnung*
4  **to put one's hands on one's hips** - *die Arme in die Seite stemmen*
5  **to pause for thought** – *kurz nachdenken*
6  **free** – hier: *gratis*
7  **to jump** – hier: *erschrecken*
8  **to tip** – *ausschütten*
9  **entire** – *ganz*
10  **to swear** – *fluchen, schimpfen*

to do. Then I think of something. I smile my best girly smile and say in my best girly voice, "I'm a fan of his. I'd like an autograph¹!"

Both boys snort and laugh.

"When you've finished laughing, maybe you could go and get him?" I say coolly.

"Oh, why of course²!" they say and disappear, still laughing, into the changing rooms. I'm annoyed – they're a year younger than me, damn it, they should show some respect. I can hear them talking to Oliver through the door.

"Hey, Olli! You've got a fan waiting out there!" shouts one of them.

"Fan? She's more of a groupie," says the other one, "and she seems pretty desperate to³ meet you – like, she's asking everyone who goes out there if he's Oliver."

I'm outraged⁴. What's all that about?⁵ How did these dwarves⁶ get the idea that ... Oh yeah, because I told them so. Oh no, that was such a stupid idea! I should have gone with the free hotdog⁷.

· · · · · · · · ·
1 **autograph** – *Autogramm*
2 **Why of course!** – *Ja, gern!*
3 **desperate to** – *wild darauf*
4 **outraged** – *empört*
5 **What's all that about?** – *Was soll denn das?*
6 **dwarf** – *Zwerg*
7 **I should have gone with the free hotdog.** (Umgangssprache) – *Ich hätte besser die Sache mit dem Gratishotdog erzählen sollen.*

60

The fact that I can hear every word they're saying is not just down to them speaking so loudly [1]; I also have my ear pressed to the door, and this in turn means that I almost go tumbling in [2] as one of the boys opens the door.

> Love-Question 2
> ☑ INBOX
> from: Jojo Mobile
>
> I can't believe I'm doing this! These boys r so stupid. How is it going with Sara?

"Damn it! Can't you knock first [3]?" I shout. Then I realise that this comment is completely out of place [4]; but since I look so angry and the boy is kind of frightened, he mumbles, "Sorry" and continues on his way. I quickly step back from the door and the discussion inside continues. Now that the door is ajar [5], I can better understand what's being said – not that I really want to hear it.

"She's crazy for you!"

"She's been out there waiting for an hour!"

"She's serious [6], man."

"I'd be careful of that girl [7], Olli. You poor thing."

For God's sake! They're making this guy afraid of me [8]. I'm about to go in and tell them all what I think. Now, Oliver doesn't want

· · · · · · · · ·

1 **not just down to them speaking so loudly** - *liegt nicht nur daran, dass sie so laut sprechen*
2 **to go tumbling in** - *der Länge nach hineinfallen*
3 **Can't you knock first?** - *Kannst du nicht anklopfen?*
4 **out of place** - *fehl am Platz, unpassend*
5 **ajar** - *etwas offen*
6 **She's serious** - *Die meint's ernst*
7 **I'd be careful of that girl!** - *Vor der würde ich mich in Acht nehmen!*
8 **to make sb. afraid** - *jdn. einschüchtern*

to come out, but it would seem that the two boys don't want to miss out on the fun¹ and they drag² him out. They're stood on either side of him and are holding his upper arms tight³ as they deposit⁴ him in front of me. Oliver tries to turn back. Somehow it's not the best start. I pretend⁵ that I don't notice how strange⁶ this is, though.

"Hi Oliver," I say, smiling at him. The lads⁷ are laughing themselves silly⁸. They can't stop. I roll my eyes⁹. This could really get difficult. "Do you fancy¹⁰ a hotdog?" I finally ask. I've thought about it and it doesn't matter if I actually come with him to the stand: I just need to get him there. I'll go with him and then turn back at the last minute¹¹, before the hotdog guys sees me.

Oliver has, in the meantime, shaken off¹² the other two. He looks at me. "You're not my type," he says and goes back into the changing rooms. What a cheek!¹³ Is he barking mad?¹⁴

I go storming after him¹⁵. "I didn't ask if I was your type or not! I a

· · · · · · · · ·

1 **to miss out on the fun** – *sich den Spaß nehmen lassen*
2 **to drag** – *schleppen*
3 **to hold tight** – *festhalten*
4 **to deposit** – *abstellen*
5 **to pretend** – *so tun, als ob*
6 **strange** – *merkwürdig*
7 **lads** (Umgangssprache) – *Jungs*
8 **to laugh oneself silly** (Umgangssprache) – *sich kaputtlachen*
9 **to roll one's eyes** – *die Augen verdrehen*
10 **to fancy something** – *Lust auf etw. haben*
11 **at the last minute** – *im letzten Moment*
12 **to shake off** – *abschütteln*
13 **What a cheek!** – *Frechheit!*
14 **Is he barking mad?** – *Spinnt der?*
15 **to storm after someone** – *jdm. hinterher stürmen*

sked if you wanted a hotdog!" I shout.

Oliver ducks back[1], clearly scared. Ha! I bet he didn't expect that[2]! Me, in the changing rooms! He probably thought he was safe here; and, in reality, he kind of should be safe here. This is, after all, the boys' changing rooms. I stop short[3]. I really should have thought this through before storming in; suddenly, I'm pretty embarrassed – mainly[4] because everyone is staring at me[5]. A couple of the boys in the changing rooms yell[6] at me to get out. A few others scream[7] like girls and run away.

Oliver's two friends shout over to me, "Great chat-up technique[8]! You just don't give in[9]!"

Oliver seems to find the whole thing very unpleasant[10]. He looks at me, frightened, and shouts, "Just leave me alone!"

I'm no longer up for diplomacy and little games, so I pull him aside and have a go at him[11].

"Listen, you idiot! I'm not in the least[12] interested in you, just to make that clear. But there's this strange girl who is supposed to

· · · · · · · · ·

1 **to duck back** – *zurückweichen*
2 **I bet he didn't expect that!** – *Damit hat er wohl nicht gerechnet!*
3 **to stop short** – *stutzen*
4 **mainly** – *vor allem*
5 **to stare at sb.** – *jdn. anstarren*
6 **to yell** – *brüllen*
7 **to scream** – hier: *quietschen*
8 **chat-up technique** – *Anmache*
9 **You just don't give in!** (Umgangssprache) – *Du bist echt hartnäckig!*
10 **unpleasant** – *unangenehm*
11 **to have a go at sb.** – *jdn. anfauchen*
12 **in the least** – *im Geringsten*

fancy you[1] and my romance-addict of a friend[2] wants us to play Cupid and get you two hooked up!"

Yes, I know, there are more elegant methods, but everything has gone so wrong that the only way forward is to go all-out[3]. "So get moving!" I shout.

"No. And get out of the changing rooms!"

"Listen, if you don't come with me now, I might have to resort to other means[4]. You should know that I have a black band – or whatever it's called – in karate." I know that Cupid doesn't necessarily use this kind of trick but, hey, Oliver would be a tough case[5] even for him.

Oliver looks at me, surprised. Either he doesn't believe me or he really is afraid.

"It's called a black belt," he says by way of correcting me.

"Yeah, whatever," I say, waving my hand, "now, the one who likes you is the one dressed in black with long dark hair and glasses – she was smiling at you the whole game. She really likes you," I say by way of reconciliation[6].

"Seriously?" says Oliver, looking astonished[7]. Bingo! It looks like we're in business[8].

"Yes, seriously. Now come on, silly!"

· · · · · · · · ·

1 **to fancy sb.** – *jdn. süß finden*
2 **my romance-addict of a friend** – *meine romantiksüchtige Freundin*
3 **to go all-out** – *auf Haruck-Methoden zurückgreifen*
4 **to resort to other means** – *zu anderen Mitteln greifen*
5 **tough case** – *schwieriger Fall*
6 **by way of reconciliation** – *versöhnlich*
7 **astonished** – *erstaunt*
8 **It looks like we're in business.** (Umgangssprache) – *Es scheint aufzugehen.*

TR. 05 I should be proud of myself[1]. I've managed to land[2] the man of Sara's dreams and I'm now taking him to the hotdog stand. Nevertheless, the long and tough battle to get him to come has made me more an-

> Love-Question 3
> ☑ INBOX
> from: Lucilla Mobile
>
> Jojo! What r u doing?
> Where r u guys? Text
> back now!

noyed than anything[3]. With some distance still to go[4] to the hot-dog stand, I stop. What to do now? I can't very well[5] just shove[6] him in front of Sara, say 'There you go! Enjoy!' and then run off. Hm. Oliver stands still and looks at me. Lucilla is already stand-ing there with Sara waiting and, I must say, she's done a good job. Sara looks pretty cool with styled hair, no glasses and, yes, green really is her colour. Lucilla was right – the T-shirt looks good on her.

I consider[7] my strategy. I need one. Hm. We could do it all nice and cool[8]. I turn to Oliver. "Listen up, I know what we'll do. Go and stand next to Sara ..."

"She's called Sara?" he asks and goes red. Great! All you have to do is say her name and he blushes[9]. This could be tough.

"Yes. Don't interrupt[10]. So, you go and stand next to Sara, then I'll come along and we'll pretend that we don't know each other ..."

. . . . . . . . .

1 **proud of oneself** – *stolz auf sich*
2 **to land** – *an Land ziehen*
3 **more annoyed then anything** – *eher genervt*
4 **with some distance still to go** – *noch in einiger Entfernung*
5 **I can't very well...** – *Ich kann ja wohl schlecht...*
6 **to shove** – *schubsen*
7 **to consider** – *überlegen*
8 **nice and cool** – *lässig*
9 **to blush** – *erröten*
10 **to interrupt** – *unterbrechen*

"Why, when we already know each other?"

"No, we don't know each other. And this little episode will be forgotten[1] quickly – very quickly. Anyway, go over there and wait for me."

I'm hoping that, once he's there, Lucilla will take over[2] and I'm out of the whole mess – without getting into trouble with[3] the hotdog guy. But Oliver isn't moving.

"What is it? Are you too scared?"

"She's not there," he says.

"Who?"

"Sara. She's nowhere to be seen.[4]"

"What are you talking about?" I laugh and point to Lucilla and Sara.

"No, she's not there. All I can see are two puffed-up[5] fashion queens[6]. The girl I saw looked completely different – she was quiet, you wouldn't have noticed her[7]. She had a kind of serious, almost sad face."

I look at him, wide-eyed[8]. You've got to be joking![9] He preferred her *before* Lucilla's make-over?

"And you like them like that?"[10] I ask.

· · · · · · · · ·

1 **will be forgotten** – *wird vergessen werden*
2 **to take over** – *die Führung übernehmen*
3 **to get into trouble with sb.** – *Ärger kriegen mit jdm.*
4 **nowhere to be seen** – *nirgends zu sehen*
5 **puffed-up** – *aufgeblasen*
6 **fashion queen** (umgangsprachlich) – *Modetussi*
7 **You wouldn't have noticed her.** – *Sie war eher unauffällig.*
8 **wide-eyed** – *mit aufgerissenen Augen*
9 **You've got to be joking!** (Redewendung) – *Du machst Witze!*
10 **You like them like that?** (Umgangssprache) – *So was findest du toll?*

"Of course," replies Oliver and looks at me as if I'm mad for asking the question.

"Oh no!"

"What's the problem now?" asks Oliver.

I don't know! I mean, we've got Lucilla working her magic[1] to turn this dowdy wall-flower into a cool girl, and then ... and then this![2] What a mess![3] And I can't even discuss[4] the situation with Lucilla, I've got to do something. Now.

Oliver looks at me expectantly[5].

"Where is Sara?" he asks. I have to think of something; I start to speak, although I don't know how I'm going to end my sentence[6].

"Er ... well, the thing is ... er ... Sara is ... not there yet!"

Hm. That doesn't really help us out. I look at Sara: she really does look completely different and, honestly, a lot more attractive; but not to Oliver's eyes. After all, he doesn't even recognise her. How can I get us the 'old' Sara? Oliver looks down at his watch.

"I've only got ten minutes, then we've got a team strategy talk with our trainer, and I don't have any idea how long that will last."

I look at Oliver kind of absently[7] for a moment. Then I get the perfect idea!

· · · · · · · · · ·

1 **to work one's magic** – *den Zauberstab schwenken, seine ganze Kunst anwenden*
2 **And then this!** – *Und jetzt so was!*
3 **What a mess!** – *Was für ein Mist! Das ist echt nach hinten losgegangen!*
4 **to discuss** – *besprechen*
5 **expectantly** – *abwartend*
6 **to end a sentence** – *einen Satz beenden*
7 **absently** – *geistesabwesend*

"Ten minutes? Great, that's fine. Wait here just a sec[1], then go to the hotdog stand and wait. I'll bring Sara and, once I come back with her, I'll introduce you two. Alright?"

TR. 06 Right. I breathe deeply because, from now on, everything is going to happen quickly. Not just because of Oliver, but because of hotdog guy – I'm not up for listening to another sermon[2] from him. So I run to the stand, grab Sara and shout to Lucilla, "No time to explain! Come with me!" Then I pull Sara, who is completely confused[3], away from the stand towards the girls' changing rooms.

Lucilla comes shouting after us. "Jojo, what are you doing? Have you gone nuts[4]?"

"I'm barred[5] from the hotdog stand. I completely forgot to tell you that and, by the way ..." I hesitate, I don't want to tell Sara that Oliver doesn't recognise her. Lucilla isn't helping.

"For God's sake! Why do you always have to turn everything into complete chaos?" she shouts.

"I'm clearing up after chaos right now!" I reply, manoeuvre[6] Sara into the changing rooms, shove her in front of the mirror:

"Take that make-up off[7]," I command[8], "quickly! We don't have much time!"

• • • • • • • • •

1 **just a sec** (Umgangssprache) – *Augenblick, zwei Sekunden*
2 **sermon** – *Predigt*
3 **confused** – *verblüfft*
4 **Have you gone nuts?** (Umgangssprache) – *Spinnst du? Hast du sie noch alle?*
5 **to be barred** – *Hausverbot haben*
6 **to manoeuvre** – hier: *bugsieren*
7 **to take off make-up** – *sich abschminken*
8 **to command** – *befehlen*

"Why ...?" she asks.

"Oliver didn't ... er ... he ... he likes girls who look depressed."

"What do you mean by that?" [1]

"Listen, Oliver is waiting for you at the hotdog stand; you don't need any more information right now. Now, get that make-up off!"

Sara is completely lost [2], but does what she's told. As she's removing her make-up, I take her hair down.

Lucilla goes crazy, "Jojo, what the hell are you doing? Do you know how much effort that took [3]?"

"It's a great hairstyle, it looks great, but ..."

I pull Lucilla away, lean close to her and whisper in her ear.

"Sara's Romeo doesn't like that sort of thing [4]."

"Romeo?" says Lucilla, "you were supposed to get Oliver!"

"I know. I ... er ... never mind. Look, the point is [5], Oliver liked Sara how she was before. He didn't even recognise your new-and-improved [6] Sara!"

"You mean to say that ..." Lucilla looks completely blank. "You mean ..." Then she stops and shakes her head: "I don't believe it!" [7]

I shrug my shoulders and start looking for Sara's black T-shirt in Lucilla's bag; I find it, run over to Sara and hand it to her.

"Come on, quickly, put this back on," I say, tearing at the green T-shirt while still talking.

. . . . . . . . .

1 **What do mean by that?** – *Was soll denn das heißen?*
2 **lost** – hier: *irritiert*
3 **to take effort** – *Mühe machen*
4 **that sort of thing** – *dergleichen, so etwas*
5 **the point is...** – *kurz gesagt, der Punkt ist...*
6 **new-and-improved** – *verbessert*
7 **I don't believe it!** – *Das gibt's doch nicht!*

After a couple of minutes, the old Sara is back. Lucilla, now in a bad mood, even hands her back her glasses; Sara puts them back on and is her old self again[1]: dark, unassuming[2], a veil of mistrust over her eyes[3].

"Perfect!" I say, beaming[4]. Lucilla turns away, visibly upset[5]. I grab Sara and drag her back out, Lucilla following angrily behind[6] us as we head for[7] the hotdog stand.

"What the hell is going on here?" asks Sara.

"Never mind," I say and wave my hand. Then I smile at her, "Your Prince Oliver is already waiting for you at the hotdog stand!"

Now, however, we see the hotdog stand – and Oliver isn't there! Damn it! I look at Sara blankly.

"I don't get it[8]. I told him very clearly to …" As I speak, Sara looks scared.

"What did you tell him?" she asks, "you didn't tell him about me, did you?"

"Of course not! What kind of idiot would do something like that[9]?"

Lucilla gives me a sideways look[10], full of mistrust[11], with a look in her eyes that says, "You! You're the kind of idiot who would do something like that." And she'd be right, unfortunately. I'm

· · · · · · · · ·

1 **to be one's old self again** – *wieder man selbst sein*
2 **unassuming** – *unscheinbar*
3 **a veil of mistrust over her eyes** – *mit missmutigem Blick*
4 **beaming** – *strahlend*
5 **visibly upset** – *augenscheinlich aufgebracht*
6 **following angrily behind** – *verärgert hinterherlaufend*
7 **To head for sth.** – *sich die in Richtung von etw. auf den Weg machen*
8 **I don't get it.** (Umgangssprache) – *Das versteh ich nicht.*
9 **What kind of idiot would do something like that?** – *Wer wäre denn so bescheuert, so etwas zu tun?*
10 **to give someone a sideways look** – *jdn. von der Seite ansehen*
11 **full of mistrust** – *misstrauisch*

not a great candidate for secret missions[1] or diplomatic affairs[2].

"Well, what did you tell him? You didn't tell him that I fancy him, did you?" asks Sara with panic in her voice.

"No, I told him that I fancy him and that he should meet me there. So I don't understand why he's not there," I said, wondering out loud[3].

"Well, he probably didn't want to meet *you*," says Sara cheekily[4], "and I don't want to spend any more time hanging around with you nutters[5] either", she continues. She moans, groans[6], swears at us and then disappears.

TR. 07  Lucilla looks at me angrily, "You've ruined everything! Again! What the hell were you thinking? It was all going so well!"

"Nothing was going well, Lucilla. Oliver didn't like the new Sara, so I had to change her back[7]!"

"Oh, yeah, and then he's not there anyway. So it was all for nothing[8]!"

I shrug my shoulders.

"I have the sinking feeling[9] that everything is your fault," says Lucilla, giving me a sideways look. I too have that feeling, but I think it's probably just the force of habit[10] - everyone, including

· · · · · · · · ·

1 **secret missions** – *geheime Missionen*
2 **diplomatic affairs** – *diplomatische Angelegenheiten*
3 **to wonder out loud** – *über etw. laut nachdenken*
4 **cheekily** – *frech*
5 **nutter** (Umgangssprache) – *Verrückte(r)*
6 **to moan, to groan** – *meckern, murren*
7 **to change sth./sb. back** – *zurückverwandeln*
8 **for nothing** – *umsonst*
9 **sinking feeling** – *ungutes Gefühl*
10 **force of habit** – *Macht der Gewohnheit*

me, blames me[1] automatically the minute anything goes wrong. "We shouldn't stick our noses into other people's business[2]. It was a stupid idea." Lucilla sighs as she talks and looks at me reproachfully[3].

"Hey, it wasn't my idea!" I say in my defence.

"Oh, don't worry about it," says Lucilla, comforting me[4], "you learned something from this experience."

"Yes, I sure did, never to listen to you."

"Jojo," says Lucilla thoughtfully[5], "you still don't have a clue[6] about romance." I'm about to reply and then I decide to stop. That's just the way Lucilla is[7] - Lucilla and her Lucilla-logic. There is no way round that[8].

We're quite sad as we walk over to the ice-cream stand[9]. We buy ourselves ice-cream and then sit down on a bench behind the stand.

"How did it go with Oliver then? Did you talk to him at all?" asks Lucilla.

"Well of course! It was easy," I say, thinking that it won't do any harm to leave out the more embarrassing details, "and he really was going to[10] come to the hotdog stand."

· · · · · · · ·

1 **to blame sb.** – *jdm. die Schuld geben*
2 **to stick one's nose into other people's business** – *sich in das Leben anderer einmischen*
3 **reproachfully** – *vorwurfsvoll*
4 **to comfort sb.** – *jdn. trösten*
5 **thoughtfully** – *nachsichtig*
6 **to not have a clue about sth.** – *von etw. keine Ahnung haben*
7 **that's just the way Lucilla is** – *so ist Lucilla eben*
8 **there is no way round that** – *dagegen kommt man nicht an.*
9 **ice-cream stand** – *Eisstand*
10 **He really was going to ...** – *Er wollte wirklich ...*

"And are you sure," asks Lucilla doubtingly[1], "that you haven't done anything, like, chaotic or embarrassing?"

"No! Why would you think that?" I grumble[2] and go slightly red. Lucilla grabs my arm so suddenly[3] that my scoop of ice-cream[4] falls out of the cone and onto my trousers.

"Did you hear that?" whispers Lucilla.

"What?" I grumble, trying to manoeuvre the scoop of ice-cream back onto the cone, which seems to be making the stain[5] on my trousers bigger.

Lucilla looks down and, shaking her head[6], asks, "What are you doing now?"

Before I get the chance to reply, though, she puts her finger to her lips by way of asking me to be quiet. Then she stands up, creeps[7] to the ice-cream stand and peeps[8] carefully around the corner. She's back in a second, grabbing my arm and pulling me up[9] - this leads to my ice-cream cone dropping to the floor once and for all[10]. She drags me behind the ice-cream stand, pushes herself against the wall and eavesdrops[11] for all she's worth[12].

"What are we doing here?" I ask.

"We're listening," she whispers.

· · · · · · · · · ·

1 **doubtingly** – *zweifelnd*
2 **to grumble** – *knurren*
3 **suddenly** – *plötzlich*
4 **scoop of ice-cream** – *Eiskugel*
5 **stain** – *Fleck*
6 **shaking her head** – *kopfschüttelnd*
7 **to creep** – *schleichen*
8 **to peep** – *heimlich gucken*
9 **to pull sb. up** – *jdn. in die Höhe reißen*
10 **once and for all** – *endgültig*
11 **to eavesdrop** – *lauschen*
12 **for all one is worth** (Umgangssprache) – *angestrengt, was das Zeug hält*

"To who? The birds twittering? The wind rustling in the leaves?" I whisper to our Queen of Romance, slightly annoyed by all of this. Then I pause for a second and cock my ears, Lucilla nods at me expressively[1]. From here we can hear the conversation in front of the ice-cream stand, and I think I know one of the voices.

"Which flavour[2] do you want? Wait, I know, you want chocolate, right?" asks the voice.

"You're amazing Oliver; how did you know that?"

"It's the darkest colour they have, and you like dark colours," says Oliver.

"You don't think they've ..." I say, looking at Lucilla. Lucilla nods eagerly[3].

"It's them! Isn't that great?! So they have got together! Ha! True love conquers all obstacles[4]."

So it would seem. Not even Lucilla's attempts at matchmaking[5] managed to hold it up[6].

"And think about it – they owe it all to us[7]!" whispers Lucilla, beaming.

Our two little turtledoves[8] seem to be getting along like a house on fire[9]. They are chatting and laughing along without a moment's silence.

· · · · · · · · ·

1 **expressively** – *ausdrucksvoll, vielsagend*
2 **flavour** – *Geschmack, Sorte*
3 **eagerly** – *eifrig*
4 **true love conquers all obstacles** – *wahre Liebe lässt sich nicht aufhalten*
5 **attempts at matchmaking** – *Verkuppelungsversuche*
6 **to hold sth. up** – *etw. aufhalten*
7 **They owe it all to us.** – *Das haben sie alles nur uns zu verdanken.*
8 **turtle dove** – *Turteltaube*
9 **to get along like a house on fire** (Redewendung) – *sich sehr gut verstehen*

"Isn't it funny that we got to know each other at the hotdog stand, although we're both vegetarian?" says Sara happily.

"Hotdog stand?" I say, looking at Lucilla, "how did that happen? He wasn't there and she went running off."

"Well, they probably both came back after we'd left. Ah, the course of true love never did run smooth[1]."

"Yes, very funny," said Oliver to Sara, "but that was due to the fact that this Jojo girl wouldn't shut up about the hotdog stand, and so I thought to myself 'go and take a look at it'." I look triumphantly at Lucilla. So, who's a regular little Cupid then[2]? Lucilla nods in acknowledgement[3].

"Honestly," continues Oliver, "you should have seen the act she put on! She even came storming into the boys' changing rooms and had a go at me because I'd told her outside to leave me alone and that she wasn't my type. But she just didn't give up; it was so embarrassing. The lads are still laughing about her now."

"Some girls are just unbearable[4]," says Sara, "I've already heard all about this girl Jojo ..."

Lucilla looks at me angrily and shouts at me as quietly as she can, "Haven't I told you to pull yourself together and behave normally? I don't want to have to change schools because of you." Well, that's not going to help much, I thought to myself, because I'm already known as the "chaos queen" at other schools, too. I was quite ready to admit I was wrong[5], but first and foremost[6] I was outraged about this cheeky guy and Sara's rudeness.

• • • • • • • • •

1 **The course of true love never did run smooth** – *Ach, die Wege der Liebe...*
2 **So who's a regular little Cupid then?** – *Da soll noch einer sagen, ich kann nicht Amor spielen.*
3 **acknowledgement** – *Anerkennung*
4 **unbearable** – *unerträglich, wie die Pest*
5 **ready to admit I was wrong** – *bereit, meinen Fehler einzusehen*
6 **first and foremost** – *in erster Linie*

"This bad-tempered Sara of yours is a right cow[1]!" I shout at Lucilla – I have to let out my anger on someone[2].

"Stop having a go at Sara when it's you who's been an idiot!" replies Lucilla. Then, however, we hear Sara continue.

" ... But the worst is Lucilla. Oh my God! She's a complete freak[3]! I could tell you some stuff about that girl that would really make you laugh!"

Now it's Lucilla who's outraged. She clenches her fist[4] and hisses, "Wow! She really *is* a cow!" It looks as if she were about to[5] shoot round the corner and lay into Sara[6]. I pull her away from the ice-cream stand and try to calm her down[7]. We go back to the seats.

"That's the last time I'm ever going to try and help anyone," shouts Lucilla angrily.

"I hope so!" I say, nodding.

"You really try to help, do everything you can[8] - and this is what you get for it! A complete waste of time.[9]

"Hey, that's not true," I shout, "it worked, didn't it? They've met and they're talking to each other."

Lucilla looks at me and suddenly a wide smile spreads across her face, "Yes, you're right. Jojo, we're the best! We actually managed to play Cupid!" she cheers[10].

· · · · · · · · ·

1 **a right cow** (Umgangssprache) - *eine dumme Zicke, eine blöde Kuh*
2 **to let out anger on sb.** - *Wut an jdm. auslassen*
3 **to be a freak** - *ein Rad ab haben*
4 **to clench one's fist** - *die Faust ballen*
5 **to be about to do sth.** - *kurz davor sein, etw. zu tun*
6 **to lay into** - *jdn. anschnauzen, sich jdn. vorknöpfen*
7 **to calm sb. down** - *jdn. beruhigen*
8 **to do everything one can** - *sich jede erdenkliche Mühe geben*
9 **A complete waste of time!** - *Alles für die Katz!*
10 **to cheer** - *jubeln*

"Well," I say, trying to curb her enthusiasm [1], "it was pretty ropy [2]. I don't know whether Cupid would give us a job in his company."
"Yes," says Lucilla nodding, "you could have been more elegant about it."

As the last game begins, Lucilla and I go back to our seats on the stand. We've only just sat down when a girl we've never met [3] starts talking to us, "Hey, I hear you guys have got this kind of like [4] dating agency going! I need your help – I'd really like to get to know the outside right on your school's team. Can you sort that out for me?"
"No!" I shout, horrified [5].
"Of course!" shouts Lucilla, enthusiastically.

1 **to curb sb.'s enthusiasm** – *jdns. Enthusiasmus dämpfen*
2 **ropy** (Umgangssprache) – *holprig*
3 **sb. one has never met** – *wildfremder Mensch*
4 **kind of like** (Umgangssprache) – *so eine/r*
5 **horrified** – *entsetzt*

# SMS-GLOSSAR

camera phone
Foto-Handy

inbox
Eingang

mobile (phone)
Handy

pay as you go
Prepaid

photo message
MMS

predictive text
Texterkennung

text sb.
jdn. ansimsen

text message
SMS

4 — for
für

2 — to; too
zu, auf; auch

2gether — together
zusammen

l8 — late
spät

w8 — wait
warten

b — be
sein

c — see
sehen

r — are
bist, sind

u — you
du, dein

ur — your; you're
dein, euer; du bist,
ihr seid

hun — honey
Schatz

gonna — going to
werden

alrite — alright/OK
OK, in Ordnung

kinda — kind of
irgendwie

wanna — want to
möchten

x - kiss
Kuss

lol - laugh out loud
laut lachend

# NÜTZLICHE AUSDRÜCKE ZUM THEMA LIEBE

| | |
|---|---|
| ask sb. out | *jdn. zu einem Date einladen* |
| be crazy / mad about sb. | *in jdn. verknallt sein* |
| be heartbroken | *todunglücklich sein* |
| be lovesick | *Liebeskummer haben* |
| chat sb. up | *jdn. anmachen* |
| chat-up line | *Anmachspruch* |
| cheat on sb. | *jdn. betrügen* |
| couple | *Pärchen* |
| dump sb. | *mit jdm. Schluss machen* |
| fall in love with sb. | *sich in jdn. verlieben* |
| have butterflies in one's stomach | *Schmetterlinge im Bauch haben* |
| hug | *sich umarmen* |
| in a relationship | *vergeben* |
| in love | *verliebt* |
| kiss | *küssen* |
| loveletter | *Liebesbrief* |
| secret note | *Geheimbotschaft* |
| single | *Single; solo* |
| shy | *schüchtern* |
| snog | *knutschen* |

# WORTLISTE

| | |
|---|---|
| A complete waste of time! | *Alles für die Katz!* |
| a cosy little chat | *ein Pläuschchen* |
| a dramatic pause | *ein Pause, um die Spannung zu erhöhen* |
| a right cow (Umgangssprache) | *eine dumme Zicke, eine blöde Kuh* |
| a veil of mistrust over her eyes | *mit misstrauischem Blick* |
| absently | *geistesabwesend* |
| acknowledgement | *Anerkennung* |
| actually | *wirklich, tatsächlich* |
| ajar | *etwas offen* |
| all of a sudden | *auf einmal* |
| amazed | *erstaunt* |
| And then follow it up with ... | *Und gleich im Anschluss komme ich mit ...* |
| And then this! | *Und jetzt so was!* |
| and while we're on the subject of waiting | *und wo wir beim Thema Warten sind* |
| angrily | *verärgert, feindselig* |
| apart from | *abgesehen von, außer* |
| apologetically | *entschuldigend* |
| as clear as clear can be | hier: *so was von klar* |
| as if it were | *als ob es wäre* |
| as if nothing has been said | *völlig unbekümmert* |
| As if you could! | *Als ob du könntest!* |
| as it happens | *wie der Zufall so will* |
| as it is | *schon, ohnehin* |
| as she puts it | *wie sie das sagt* |
| astonished | *erstaunt* |
| at least | *zumindest* |

| | |
|---|---|
| at the end of the day | *letztendlich, schließlich* |
| at the last minute | *im letzten Moment* |
| at the very least | *wenigstens, zumindest* |
| attempts at matchmaking | *Verkuppelungsversuche* |
| audibly | *hörbar* |
| autograph | *Autogramm* |
| back-up | *Reserve* |
| bad mood | *schlechte Laune* |
| bag of nerves | *Nervenbündel* |
| bark | *bellen* |
| barricaded | *verbarrikadiert* |
| bawl one's eyes out | *sich die Augen ausheulen* |
| be a freak | *ein Rad ab haben* |
| be about to do sth. | *kurz davor sein, etw. zu tun* |
| be accepted as cool | *als cool gelten* |
| be barred | *Hausverbot haben* |
| be dying to do sth. | *es kaum erwarten können, etw. zu tun* |
| be forced | hier: *verdonnert werden* |
| be meant to do sth. | *etw. tun sollen* |
| be more than enough | *dicke reichen* |
| be one's old self again | *wieder man selbst sein* |
| be over | *vorbei sein* |
| be responsible for | hier: *übernehmen* |
| be stuck | *festsitzen* |
| be taken aback | hier: *völlig perplex sein* |
| be up for sth. | *Lust auf/zu etw. haben* |
| beam | *strahlen* |
| beaming | *strahlend* |
| bearable | *erträglich* |
| beg | *betteln* |

| | |
|---|---|
| behave well | *sich gut verhalten* |
| behaviour | *Verhalten* |
| bend down | *sich bücken* |
| beside oneself | *außer sich* |
| blame oneself | *sich selbst die Schuld geben* |
| blame sb. | *jdm. die Schuld geben* |
| blankly | hier: *verständnislos* |
| blubber | *heulen* |
| blurry | *verschwommen* |
| blush | *erröten* |
| bored | *gelangweilt* |
| boring | *langweilig, unscheinbar* |
| bowled over | *sprachlos* |
| branches | *Geäst* |
| brandish | *schwenken* |
| break down in tears | *in Tränen ausbrechen* |
| breed of snail | *Schneckenzucht* |
| budding | *knospend, beginnend* |
| bug (Umgangssprache) | *nerven* |
| busy eating | *mit Essen beschäftigt* |
| But hey, who cares? | *Aber egal!* |
| But I don't know him at all. | *Aber ich kenne ihn doch gar nicht.* |
| by any chance | *zufällig* |
| by far | *bei Weitem* |
| by way of reconciliation | *versöhnlich* |
| by way of reply | *als Antwort* |
| call it a day | *einen Schlussstrich ziehen* |
| calm sb. down | *jdn. beruhigen* |
| Can't you knock first? | *Kannst du nicht anklopfen?* |
| candelabra | *Kronleuchter* |

| | |
|---|---|
| catch | hier: *fangen* |
| catch up with sb. | *jdn. einholen* |
| catwalk | *Laufsteg* |
| cautiously | *vorsichtig* |
| change sth./sb. back | *zurückverwandeln* |
| changing rooms | *Umkleide* |
| charge at | *auf jdn. losgehen* |
| chat-up technique | *Anmache* |
| cheekily | *frech* |
| cheer | *jubeln* |
| cheer sb. up | *jdn. aufmuntern* |
| cheerfully | *fröhlich* |
| chips | *Pommes frites* |
| choosy | *wählerisch* |
| clamber | *klettern* |
| classy | *vornehm, edel* |
| clench one's fist | *die Faust ballen* |
| come into consideration | *in Frage kommen* |
| comfort sb. | *jdn. trösten* |
| command | *befehlen* |
| compassionately | *mitfühlend* |
| compete against each other | *gegeneinander antreten* |
| complain | *klagen, meckern, sich beklagen* |
| completely average | *völlig unscheinbar* |
| confront sb. with sth. | *jdn. etw. vorhalten* |
| confused | *verblüfft, verwundert* |
| conquer sb.'s heart | *jdns. Herz erobern* |
| consider | *überlegen* |
| contradict | *widersprechen* |
| cookery section | *Kochbuchabteilung* |

| | |
|---|---|
| corner sb. | *jdn. stellen* |
| crack (Umgangssprache) | *durchdrehen* |
| crawl | *krabbeln* |
| crazy about sb. (Umgangssprache) | *verknallt in jdn.* |
| creep | *schleichen* |
| crumble | *bröckeln* |
| curb sb.'s enthusiasm | *jdns. Enthusiasmus dämpfen* |
| curious | *neugierig* |
| curiously | *neugierig* |
| cut sb. short | *jdm. das Wort abschneiden* |
| dangle | *baumeln* |
| deal with stuff | *sich um Dinge kümmern* |
| decide | hier: *sich festlegen* |
| deep in conversation | *im Gespräch vertieft* |
| deny | *verleugnen, zurückweisen,* |
| deposit | *abstellen* |
| despairingly | *verzweifelt* |
| desperate to | *wild darauf* |
| diplomatic affairs | *diplomatische Angelegenheiten* |
| disagree with sb. | *jdm. widersprechen* |
| discuss | *besprechen* |
| dismissively | *abweisend, wegwerfend* |
| distinguishing feature | *Unterscheidungsmerkmal* |
| distrustful | *misstrauisch* |
| do everything one can | *sich jede erdenkliche Mühe geben* |
| do stuff | *etw. unternehmen* |
| do your bit | *mach deinen Teil* |
| doable | *machbar* |
| Don't get it into your head that ... | *Denk bloß nicht, dass ...* |
| Don't overdo it! | *Übertreib's nicht!* |

| | |
|---|---|
| Don't you have something to be taking care of? | *Hast du nicht etwas zu erledigen?* |
| doubtingly | *zweifelnd* |
| drag | *schleifen, schleppen* |
| duck back | *zurückweichen* |
| due to sth. | *wegen* |
| dumbfounded | *sprachlos* |
| dump sb. | *mit jdm. Schluss machen* |
| dwarf | *Zwerg* |
| dwell on sb./sth. | *lange über jdn./etw. nachdenken* |
| eagerly | *eifrig* |
| eavesdrop | *lauschen* |
| edge | hier: *Rand* |
| embarrassing | *peinlich* |
| emphasise | *betonen* |
| encouraging | *aufmunternd* |
| end a sentence | *einen Satz beenden* |
| end up looking stupid | *am Ende blöd dastehen* |
| entire | *ganz* |
| every hour on the hour | *jede volle Stunde* |
| expectantly | *abwartend* |
| expectation | *Erwartung* |
| expressively | *ausdrucksvoll, vielsagend* |
| extravagant | *extravagant, übertrieben* |
| eye-shadow | *Lidschatten* |
| fall in love | *sich verlieben* |
| falter | *stocken* |
| fancy sb. | *jdn. süß finden* |
| fancy sth. | *Lust auf etw. haben* |
| fashion queen (Umgangssprache) | *Modetussi* |

| | |
|---|---|
| fight for sb. | *um jdn. kämpfen* |
| fighting spirit | *Kampfgeist* |
| first and foremost | *in erster Linie* |
| first off (Umgangssprache) | *als Erstes* |
| first row | *erste Reihe* |
| flavour | *Geschmack, Sorte* |
| flinch | *(zusammen)zucken* |
| Flippi doesn't mess around when it comes to acts of vengeance. | *Flippi ist nicht zimperlich, wenn es um Rache geht.* |
| fob sb. off | *jdn. abwimmeln* |
| following angrily behind | *verärgert hinterherlaufend* |
| football pitch | *Fußballplatz* |
| for ages | *seit Ewigkeiten* |
| for all one is worth (Umgangssprache) | *angestrengt, was das Zeug hält* |
| for nothing | *umsonst* |
| for once | *endlich mal* |
| for this reason alone | *allein aus diesem Grund* |
| forbidden to go anywhere near it (the stand) | *verboten, sich dem Stand künftig auch nur zu nähern* |
| force of habit | *Macht der Gewohnheit* |
| free | hier: *gratis* |
| frightened | *erschocken* |
| from every possible angle | *aus jedem erdenklichen Blickwinkel* |
| from this far off | *aus dieser Entfernung* |
| frown | *die Augenbrauen zusammenziehen* |
| full of mistrust | *misstrauisch* |
| fumble for sth. | *nach etw. tasten* |
| fundamental right | *Grundrecht* |
| furiously | *wütend* |
| gender | *Geschlecht* |

| | |
|---|---|
| gesture | *Geste* |
| get (all) worked up | *sich in etw. hineinsteigern* |
| get along like a house on fire (Redewendung) | *sich sehr gut verstehen* |
| get enthusiastic about sth. | *sich für etw. begeistern* |
| get in touch with sb. | *jdn. kontaktieren, sich bei jdm. melden* |
| get into trouble (with sb.) | *Ärger kriegen (mit jdm.), in Schwierigkeiten geraten* |
| get it over and done with | *etw. hinter sich bringen* |
| get off to a good start | *einen guten Start hinlegen* |
| get on with one's life | *sein Leben wieder in die Hand nehmen* |
| get sb. to do st. | *jdn. dazu bringen, etw. zu tun* |
| get sb.'s interest | *jdns. Interesse wecken* |
| get straight to the point | *direkt zur Sache kommen* |
| get sunburnt | *sich einen Sonnenbrand holen* |
| get the better of sb. | *die Oberhand über jdn. gewinnen* |
| get worked up about sb./sth. | *sich über jdn./etw. aufregen* |
| giggle | *kichern* |
| give sb. a grateful hug | *jdn. dankbar umarmen* |
| give sb. a nudge | *jdn. anschubsen* |
| give sb. a sideways look | *jdn. von der Seite ansehen* |
| glance | *kurz blicken* |
| go all-out | *auf Hauruck-Methoden zurückgreifen* |
| go into detail on sth. | *auf etw. eingehen* |
| go red | *rot werden* |
| go tumbling in | *der Länge nach hineinfallen* |
| go up to sb. | *zu jdm. gehen* |
| grab | *fassen, greifen, packen* |
| grasp | *begreifen* |
| grateful | *dankbar* |

| | |
|---|---|
| grin | *grinsen; Grinsen* |
| groan | *ächzen* |
| growl | *knurren* |
| gruffly | *schroff* |
| grumble | *meckern, murren; knurren* |
| guess | *raten, ahnen* |
| gulp | hier: *schlucken* |
| haircut | *Frisur* |
| half-sing | *flöten* |
| handle | *Klinke* |
| hang around with sb. | *mit jdm. abhängen* |
| hang out | *abhängen* |
| haughtily | *hochnäsig* |
| have a chat | *plaudern* |
| have a go at sb. (Umgangssprache) | *jdn. anschnauzen, anfauchen* |
| have a lump in one's throat | *einen Kloß im Hals haben* |
| have an allergy | *allergisch sein* |
| have disappeared into thin air (Redewendung) | *wie vom Erdboden verschwunden sein* |
| have it in for sb. | *es auf jdn. abgesehen haben* |
| have no business being there | *dort nichts zu suchen haben* |
| have second thoughts | *es sich anders überlegen* |
| Have you gone nuts? (Umgangssprache) | *Spinnst du?, Hast du sie noch alle?* |
| He doesn't even have the decency to try ... | *Er versucht auch nicht einmal, zu ...* |
| He really was going to ... | *Er wollte wirklich ...* |
| He's been through enough with you anyway. | *Er hat ja schon genug mit dir durchgemacht.* |

| | |
|---|---|
| head for sth. | sich die in Richtung von etw. auf den Weg machen |
| hearsay | Hörensagen |
| hedgerow | Hecke |
| hesitate | zögern |
| hiss | zischen |
| hold one's breath | den Atem anhalten |
| hold sth. up | etw. aufhalten |
| hold tight | festhalten |
| home | hier: psychiatrische Anstalt |
| honest | ehrlich |
| honestly | also wirklich |
| horrified | entsetzt |
| How come I heard all the stories from you then? | Wieso habe ich dann die ganzen Geschichten von dir gehört? |
| How low will he sink? | Wie tief kann man sinken? |
| hurry over to sb. | zu jdm. herübereilen |
| I almost died of laughter. | Ich bin fast gestorben vor Lachen. |
| I bet he didn't expect that! | Damit hat er wohl nicht gerechnet! |
| I can see this kind of thing a mile off! | So was erkenne ich aus jeder Entfernung! |
| I can't be anything except happy. | Ich bin nur noch glücklich. |
| I can't be bothered with ... (Umgangssprache) | Ich habe keine Lust auf ... |
| I can't very well... | Ich kann ja wohl schlecht ... |
| I don't believe it! | Das gibt's doch nicht! |
| I don't buy that. | Das glaub ich kaum.; Das glaub ich dir nicht. |
| I don't care about anything else! | Alles andere ist mir egal! |
| I don't get it. (Umgangssprache) | Das versteh ich nicht. |

| | |
|---|---|
| I grabbed what I thought was the suntan lotion. | *Ich griff nach dem, was ich für die Sonnenmilch hielt.* |
| I have no other choice but... | *Mir bleibt nichts anderes übrig, als ...* |
| I haven't seen you for ages. | *Lange nicht mehr gesehen.* |
| I just manage to stop myself. | *Ich bekomme es gerade noch hin, mich wieder einzukriegen.* |
| I keep walking along beside Lucilla. | *Ich laufe weiter neben Lucilla her.* |
| I might as well talk to him. | *Kann ich auch mit ihm reden.* |
| I might just as well have kept going to school. | *Ich hätte genauso gut weiterhin zur Schule gehen können.* |
| I myself think its a bit silly really. | *Ich persönlich halte es für etwas doof.* |
| I poke my head around the door. | *Ich schaue kurz zur Türe hinaus.* |
| I probably should have ended the discussion at that point ... | *Ich hätte die Diskussion an dieser Stelle beenden sollen ...* |
| I should have gone with the free hot-dog. (Umgangssprache) | *Ich hätte besser die Sache mit dem Gratishotdog erzählt.* |
| I'd be better off... | *Ich sollte lieber ...* |
| I'd be careful of that girl! | *Vor der würde ich mich in Acht nehmen!* |
| I'm supposed to help her? | *Der soll ich helfen?* |
| ice-cream parlour | *Eisdiele* |
| ice-cream stand | *Eisstand* |
| if I were you | *an deiner Stelle* |
| ignoring the fact that ... | *mal davon abgesehen, dass ...* |
| impatiently | *ungeduldig* |
| impoliteness | *Unhöflichkeit* |
| impress | *beeindrucken* |
| in an unbearably good mood | *unerträglich gut gelaunt* |
| in disbelief | *fassungslos* |
| in disgust | *angewidert* |
| in dismay | *bestürzt* |

| | |
|---|---|
| in love | *verliebt* |
| in my defence | *zu meiner Verteidigung* |
| in no relation to | *unabhängig von* |
| in the least | *im Geringsten* |
| incarceration | *Einkerkerung* |
| instruction manual | *Gebrauchsanleitung* |
| intently | *eifrig* |
| interrupt | *unterbrechen* |
| introduce oneself | *sich vorstellen* |
| invite sb. out for sth. | *jdn. zu etw. einladen* |
| Is he barking mad? | *Spinnt der?* |
| It can't go on like this! | *So geht das nicht weiter!* |
| it didn't soak into the skin at all | *sie zog überhaupt nicht in die Haut ein* |
| It looks like we're in business. (Umgangssprache) | *Es scheint aufzugehen.* |
| It was bursting at the seams. | hier: *Sie platzte aus allen Nähten.* |
| It's bound to help. | *Es wird dir auf jeden Fall helfen.* |
| It's worth a try. | *Es ist einen Versuch wert.* |
| jump | *springen;* hier: *erschrecken* |
| just a moment | *Moment mal!* |
| just a sec (Umgangssprache) | *Augenblick, zwei Sekunden* |
| just imagine | *stell dir nur vor* |
| just like that | *auf einmal, schlagartig* |
| keen on sth. | *begeistert von etw.* |
| keep | *behalten* |
| Keep cool! | *Reg dich nicht auf!, Bleib cool!* |
| keep oneself under control | *sich zusammenreißen* |
| keep sb. company | *jdm. Gesellschaft leisten* |
| keep sth. a secret from sb. | *etw. vor jdm. geheim halten* |
| keep sth. up | *mit etw. nicht aufhören* |

| | |
|---|---|
| **kind of like** (Umgangssprache) | *so eine/r* |
| **kit** | *Spielkleidung, Trikot* |
| **knit one's brow** | *die Stirn runzeln* |
| **lads** (Umgangssprache) | *Jungs* |
| **laid** | *gedeckt* |
| **land** | hier: *an Land ziehen* |
| **landing** | *(Treppen)flur* |
| **lap** | *Schoß* |
| **large letter** | *Großbuchstabe* |
| **laugh one's head off** (Redewendung) | *sich kaputtlachen* |
| **laugh oneself silly** (Umgangssprache) | *sich kaputtlachen* |
| **lay into** | *jdn. anschnauzen, sich jdn. vorknöpfen* |
| **layer** | hier: *stufen* |
| **lean one's head to one side** | *den Kopf schief legen* |
| **leave a message** | *etw. ausrichten lassen, eine Nachricht hinterlassen* |
| **Leave me alone!** | *Lass mich in Ruhe!* |
| **leave sb. in peace** | *jdn. in Frieden lassen* |
| **lecturing** | *belehrend* |
| **left over** | *übrig* |
| **leg it** (Umgangssprache) | hier: *abhauen* |
| **let out anger on sb.** | *Wut an jdm. auslassen* |
| **let sb. get a word out** | *jdn. zu Wort kommen lassen* |
| **Let us just suppose that...** | *Nehmen wir mal an, dass ...* |
| **Let's get started!** | *Legen wir mal los!* |
| **lime green** | *lindgrün* |
| **lipstick** | *Lippenstift* |
| **local championship** | *Kreismeisterschaft* |
| **longingly** | *sehnsüchtig* |
| **look after sb.** | *sich um jdn. kümmern* |

| | |
|---|---|
| look elsewhere | *sich woanders umschauen, anderweitig schauen* |
| looking very worried | *besorgt dreinschauend* |
| looks like | *sieht so aus, als ob* |
| lose (Umgangssprache) | hier: *abziehen* |
| lost | hier: *irritiert* |
| lovesick | *liebeskrank* |
| Lucilla can smell romance. | *Lucilla wittert Romantik.* |
| Lucilla has a good point there. | *Da ist was dran an dem, was Lucilla gerade gesagt hat.* |
| lure | *locken* |
| mainly | *vor allem* |
| make a mental list | *eine Liste im Kopf machen* |
| Make an effort! | *Streng dich an!* |
| make sb. afraid | *jdn. einschüchtern* |
| make-up bag | *Schminkbeutel* |
| manoeuvre | hier: *bugsieren* |
| mean | *gemein* |
| mean sb. | *jdn. meinen, von jdm. sprechen* |
| medal for bravery | *Tapferkeitsmedaille* |
| mellow sb. out (Umgangssprache) | *jdn. viel milder stimmen* |
| melt | *(dahin)schmelzen* |
| mess | *Murks, Schlamassel* |
| mind at rest | *beruhigt* |
| miserable | *übellaunig* |
| mishap | *Missgeschick* |
| miss out on the fun | *sich den Spaß nehmen lassen* |
| moan, to groan | *meckern, murren* |
| more annoyed then anything | *eher genervt* |
| move | hier: *umziehen* |

| | |
|---|---|
| mumble | *murmeln, nuscheln* |
| murmur | *murmeln, raunen* |
| my romance-addict of a friend | *meine romantiksüchtige Freundin* |
| nappy | *Windel* |
| Never heard that one before! | *Ach, wie originell!* |
| new-and-improved | *verbessert* |
| newfound courage | *neu entdeckter Mut* |
| nice and cool | *lässig* |
| Nice going! | *ironisch: Sehr geschickt!* |
| nicely avoiding embarassment | *schön ohne Peinlichkeit* |
| nightmare | *Albtraum* |
| nod | *(zustimmend) nicken* |
| not be able to stand sth. | *etw. nicht ertragen können* |
| not have a clue about sth. | *von etw. keine Ahnung haben* |
| not just down to them speaking so loudly | *liegt nicht nur daran, dass sie so laut sprechen* |
| Not on your life! | *Nie im Leben!* |
| notice | *merken* |
| notoriously | *notorisch* |
| now of all times | *ausgerechnet jetzt* |
| Now that's just going too far! | *Das geht jetzt aber zu weit!* |
| Now, off you go! | *Nun geh schon!* |
| nowhere to be seen | *nirgends zu sehen* |
| nudge | *Schubs* |
| nutter (Umgangssprache) | *Verrückte(r)* |
| occasionally | *hin und wieder* |
| oh, right | *ach so, aha* |
| once and for all | *endgültig* |
| one big disaster | *eine einzige Katastrophe* |
| or rather | *beziehungsweise* |

| | |
|---|---|
| or something like that | *oder so* |
| Oskar only just about manages ... | *Oskar schafft es gerade noch ...* |
| out of place | *fehl am Platz, unpassend* |
| out of play | *aus* |
| outraged | *empört* |
| overcome with remorse | *völlig zerknirscht* |
| owe sb. sth. | *jdm. etw. schuldig sein* |
| pat | *klopfen* |
| patience of a saint | *Engelsgeduld* |
| pause for thought | *kurz nachdenken* |
| peep | *heimlich gucken* |
| peer cautiously | *heimlich/zögernd spähen* |
| peer out | hier: *spähen* |
| phased (Umgangssprache) | *aus dem Konzept gebracht* |
| pillow | *Kopfkissen* |
| pity | *Mitleid* |
| play Cupid | *Amor spielen* |
| pool | hier: *Freibad* |
| pour out one's heart to sb. | *jdm. seine ganze Leidensgeschichte erzählen* |
| precious | *wertvoll* |
| prefer ketchup | *lieber Ketchup mögen* |
| prefer sth. | *etw. vorziehen* |
| prepared | *vorbereitet* |
| pretend | *so tun als ob* |
| pretty obvious | *völlig klar* |
| previous | *vorhergehende* |
| professional | *fachkundig, dienstlich, geschäftsmäßig* |
| profits | *Gewinn* |
| proof of love | *Liebesbeweis* |

| | |
|---|---|
| proud of oneself | *stolz auf sich* |
| public nuisance | *Nervensäge, Störenfried* |
| puffed-up | *aufgeplustert* |
| pull a face | *ein Gesicht ziehen* |
| pull sb. aside | *jdn. zur Seite ziehen* |
| pull sb. up | *jdn. in die Höhe reißen* |
| put on sth. | *mit etw. um die Ecke kommen* |
| put one's hands on one's hips | *die Arme in die Seite stemmen* |
| put sth. behind oneself | *über etw. hinwegkommen* |
| quite fancy sth. | *ziemliche Lust auf etw. haben* |
| quite honestly | *ehrlich gesagt* |
| racked with doubt | *von Zweifeln geplagt* |
| ready to admit I was wrong | *bereit, meinen Fehler einzugestehen* |
| realise | *merken* |
| really annoyed about sth. | *über etw. total sauer* |
| reasonable | *vernünftig* |
| reckon (Umgangssprache) | hier: *meinen, der Meinung sein* |
| recognise | *erkennen* |
| red-hot | *glühend heiß* |
| reel sb. in (Umgangssprache) | *jdn. an der Angel haben* |
| refuse | *sich weigern* |
| relieved | *erleichtert* |
| reproachfully | *vorwurfsvoll* |
| resistance | *Widerstand* |
| resort to other means | *zu anderen Mitteln greifen* |
| responsible | *verantwortlich* |
| restore sb.'s confidence | *das Selbstbewusstsein von jdm. wieder-herstellen* |
| restyle one's look | *sich umstylen* |
| retrieve | *borgen* |

| | |
|---|---|
| rip | *reißen* |
| **Rise and shine!** (Redewendung) | *Raus aus den Federn!* |
| roll one's eyes | *die Augen verdrehen* |
| **ropy** (Umgangssprache) | *holprig* |
| rose petals | *Rosenblüten* |
| run after sb. | *jdm. hinterherlaufen* |
| rush out | *hinausstürzen* |
| safety precaution | *Sicherheitsmaßnahme* |
| satisfied | *zufrieden* |
| sausage | *Wurst* |
| save | *retten* |
| say it to sb.'s face | *es jdm. ins Gesicht sagen* |
| sb. one has never met | *wildfremder Mensch* |
| scare sb. away | *jdn. vergraulen* |
| scare sb. off | *jdn. abschrecken, verschrecken* |
| scatter | *streuen* |
| sceptical | *skeptisch* |
| scoop of ice-cream | *Eiskugel* |
| scornfully | *verächtlich* |
| scream | hier: *quietschen* |
| scream and shout | *johlen und grölen* |
| secret missions | *geheime Missionen* |
| sedatives | *Beruhigungsmittel* |
| see sth. from the look on sb.'s face | *etw. jdm. am Gesicht ansehen* |
| seemingly | *allem Anschein nach* |
| self-inflicted | *selbst auferlegt* |
| sermon | *Predigt* |
| set to work | *mit der Arbeiten beginnen* |
| settle down | hier: *es sich bequem machen* |
| shadow | *beschatten, verfolgen* |

| | |
|---|---|
| shake off | *abschütteln* |
| shaking her head | *kopfschüttelnd* |
| She cares about you. | *Sie hat dich lieb.* |
| She's serious. | *Die meint's ernst.* |
| shove | *schubsen* |
| shriek hysterically | *hysterisch schreien* |
| shrug (one's shoulders) | *mit den Schultern zucken* |
| sigh | *seufzen* |
| sign | *Schild, Zeichen* |
| sinking feeling | *ungutes Gefühl* |
| slam the door | *die Türe zuknallen* |
| slump down the wall | *die Wand hinunterrutschen* |
| slyly | *schlau* |
| small act of clumsiness | *kleine Ungeschicklichkeit* |
| smile from ear to ear | *von einem Ohr zum anderen grinsen* |
| snap at sb. | *jdn. anschnauzen* |
| sniffle | *schniefen* |
| snort | hier: *prusten* |
| so far, so good | *so weit, so gut* |
| So get used to it! | *Dabei bleibt es und basta!* |
| So what? (Umgangssprache) | *Na und?* |
| So who's a regular little Cupid then? | *Da soll noch einer sagen, ich kann nicht Amor spielen.* |
| sob | *schluchzen* |
| Sod's Law (Redewendung) | *Murphy's Gesetz (Diese Lebensweisheit, die auf den amerikanischen Ingenieur Edward Murphy zurückgeht, besagt: „Alles was schief gehen kann, wird auch schief gehen")* |
| soften | *abmildern* |

| | |
|---|---|
| some law or other | *irgendein Gesetz* |
| **Something was up with Sven.** | *Irgendetwas war mit Sven.* |
| sound like sth. | *nach/wie etw. klingen* |
| spare | *Wechsel-, Ersatz-* |
| spread out | *ausbreiten* |
| squeak | *quieken* |
| stack | *Stapel* |
| stain | *Fleck* |
| stalk | hier: *marschieren, sich stürzen* |
| stamp | *stampfen* |
| stare at sb. | *jdn. anstarren* |
| step-by-step | *Schritt für Schritt* |
| stern | *streng, unnachgiebig* |
| **Something must have happened.** | *Irgendetwas muss geschehen sein.* |
| stick one's nose into other people's business | *sich in das Leben anderer einmischen* |
| stony face | *versteinerte Miene* |
| stop dead in one's tracks (Redewendung) | *wie angewurzelt stehen bleiben* |
| stop short | *stutzen* |
| storm after sb. | *jdm. hinterher stürmen* |
| straight afterwards | *direkt im Anschluss* |
| strange | *merkwürdig* |
| strangle | *erwürgen* |
| stretch | hier: *sich erstrecken* |
| strictly | *steng* |
| string | *Schnur, Bindfaden* |
| strut | *stolzieren* |
| stubbornly | *trotzig, hartnäckig* |
| stumble into sb. | hier: *in jdn. hineinstolpern* |

| | |
|---|---|
| successor | *Nachfolger* |
| such a sweetie | *sooo süß* |
| suddenly | *plötzlich* |
| suffer | *leiden* |
| sugary | *zuckersüß* |
| suntan lotion | *Sonnenmilch* |
| suspiciously | *misstrauisch* |
| swallow | *schlucken* |
| swear | *fluchen, schimpfen* |
| tablecloth | *Tischdecke* |
| take a deep breath | *tief Luft holen* |
| take a sip | *einen kleinen Schluck nehmen* |
| take effort | *Mühe machen* |
| take off make-up | *sich abschminken* |
| take over | *die Führung übernehmen* |
| take sth. hard | *etw. schwernehmen* |
| Talk about stupid! | *Wie dumm kann man bitte sein?* |
| teeny-weeny (Umgangssprache) | *klitzeklein* |
| tell sb. sth. to his face | *jdm. etw. ins Gesicht sagen* |
| tense up | *sich versteifen, sich anspannen* |
| that sort of thing | *dergleichen, so etwas* |
| That will teach Lucilla! | *Das geschieht Lucilla auch recht!* |
| That's a promise! | *Garantiert!* |
| That's a recipe for disaster. (Redewendung) | *Da ist die Katastrophe schon vorprogrammiert.* |
| That's how you can tell he's captain. | *Daran erkennst du, dass er Kapitän ist.* |
| That's just the way Lucilla is. | *So ist Lucilla eben.* |
| The course of true love never did run smooth. | *Ach, die Wege der Liebe…* |
| The fact that I end up… | *Die Tatsache, dass ich letztendlich …* |

| the first signs | die ersten Zeichen/Ansätze |
|---|---|
| the honourable art of suffering | hier: *die hohe Kunst des Leidens* |
| the ones that have fallen on the floor | *die Runtergefallenen* |
| the point is... | *kurz gesagt ..., der Punkt ist ...* |
| the really keen ones | *die ganz Eifrigen* |
| the right order | *die richtige Reihenfolge* |
| the slightest idea | *die geringste Ahnung* |
| Their eyes met. | *Ihre Blicke haben sich gekreuzt.* |
| There are so many other nice boys around. | *Es gibt so viele andere nette Jungs.* |
| There is no way round that. | *Dagegen kommt man nicht an.* |
| They all look the same. | *Die sehen alle gleich aus.* |
| They owe it all to us. | *Das haben sie alles nur uns zu verdanken.* |
| think again about sth. | *sich etw. nochmal überlegen* |
| think out loud | *laut denken* |
| This guy really has a nerve. | *Der Typ hat vielleicht Nerven.* |
| This is the worst bit. | *Jetzt kommt das Schlimmste.* |
| thoughtfully | *nachsichtig* |
| throw-in | *Einwurf* |
| tip | *schütten* |
| top | hier: *Oberteil* |
| totally embarassing | *oberpeinlich* |
| touched | *gerührt* |
| tough | hier: *hart* |
| tough case | *schwieriger Fall* |
| tracksuit | *Trainingsanzug* |
| trick question | *Fangfrage* |
| triumphantly | *triumphierend* |
| trouser pocket | *Hosentasche* |
| trudge on | *trotten* |

| | |
|---|---|
| True love conquers all obstacles. | *Wahre Liebe lässt sich nicht aufhalten.* |
| turn | *sich drehen* |
| turn them (two people) into a couple | *zwei Menschen verkuppeln* |
| turtle dove | *Turteltaube* |
| unassuming | *unscheinbar* |
| unbearable | *unerträglich, wie die Pest* |
| unbelievable | *unmöglich, unverschämt* |
| under the current circumstances | *unter den jetzigen Umständen* |
| unmistakeable | *untrüglich* |
| unpleasant | *unangenehm* |
| urgently | *dringend* |
| vague | *vage* |
| valuable | *wertvoll* |
| visibly upset | *augenscheinlich aufgebracht* |
| walk | hier: *Gassi* |
| wallow | *schwelgen, suhlen* |
| wardrobe | *Garderobe* |
| Was there a spark between them? | *Hat es zwischen den beiden gefunkt?* |
| wave | hier: *herumwedeln* |
| wave one's hand | *mit der Hand winken* |
| weakness | *Schwäche* |
| What a cheek! | *Frechheit!* |
| What a mess! | *Was für ein Mist!, Das ist echt nach hinten losgegangen!* |
| What do mean by that? | *Was soll denn das heißen?* |
| What kind of idiot would do something like that? | *Wer wäre denn so bescheuert, so etwas zu machen?* |
| What's all that about? | *Was soll denn das?* |
| What's that supposed to mean? | *Was soll das denn heißen?* |
| What's the matter with you? | *Was ist mit dir los?* |

| | |
|---|---|
| whingey | *weinerlich* |
| whinging | *Gejammer, Nörgelei* |
| whisper | *flüstern* |
| whoever it is | *wer auch immer es sein mag* |
| Why of course! | *Ja, gern!* |
| wide-eyed | *mit aufgerissenen Augen* |
| will be forgotten | *wird vergessen werden* |
| with one's head held high (Redewendung) | *hoch erhobenen Hauptes* |
| with some distance still to go | *noch in einiger Entfernung* |
| withdraw | hier: *sich verkriechen* |
| without batting an eyelid | *ohne mit der Wimper zu zucken* |
| without sb. noticing | *unbemerkt* |
| wonder out loud | *über etw. laut nachdenken* |
| work one's magic | *den Zauberstab schwenken, seine ganze Kunst anwenden* |
| worry about sb. | *sich um jdn. Sorgen machen* |
| Would you mind...? | *Kannst du mir bitte ...?* |
| wrist | *Handgelenk* |
| Yeah, right! | *ironisch: Ja klar!* |
| yell | *brüllen, schreien* |
| You just don't give in. (Umgangssprache) | *Du bist echt hartnäckig.* |
| You know what he's like. | *Du kennst ihn ja.* |
| You like them like that? (Umgangssprache) | *So was findest du toll?* |
| You think he's cute. | *Du findest ihn gut.* |
| You wouldn't have noticed her. | *Sie war eher unauffällig.* |
| You'd better lock the door. | *Du solltest lieber die Türe abschließen.* |

**You're bound to find another nice girl.** *Du wirst bestimmt ein anderes nettes Mädchen kennenlernen.*

**You've got to be joking!** (Redewendung) *Du machst Witze!*

## AUFGABEN

# Bliss With a Kiss

## I - MOVEMENTS OF LOVE AND PANIC

### 1. Connect
Wie sich jemand fühlt, kann man oft deutlich an Verhaltensweisen erkennen. Kannst du in den folgenden Fällen erkennen, welche Gefühle hinter dem Verhalten stecken? Verbinde die richtigen Paare.

1. to stop dead in one's tracks          _1_ A panic
2. to grab someone's arm                 _4_ B anger
3. to take a deep breath                  _3_ C fear
4. to slam the door                       _2_ D need for attention
5. to pull the bedcovers over one's head  _5_ E sorrow

### 2. Translate
Übersetze nun die Sätze 1. – 5. aus Aufgabe 1 ins Deutsche:

1. Auf der Stelle auftraren
2. Jemandens Arm greifen
3. Einen tiefen Atemzug nehmen
4. Die Tür zuschlagen
5. Die Decke über den Kopf ziehen

### 3. Complete

Wie gehen die folgenden Sätze weiter?

1. Jojo slams the door because ...
   - ☒ A she likes loud noise.
   - ☒ B she is angry and wants to be alone.
   - ☒ C she does not know how to close it quietly.

2. Sven stops dead in his tracks because ...
   - ☒ A he suddenly realises that Jojo is angry at him.
   - ☒ B his leg hurts and he cannot walk any further.
   - ☒ C he has found a dead snake.

3. Jojo pulls the bedclothes over her head because ...
   - ☒ A her room is too cold.
   - ☒ B she does not like light.
   - ☒ C she is too sad to get up.

> Im Gegensatz zum Deutschen gibt es im Englischen meistens **kein** Komma vor „because".

## 4. Odd one out

Bis zum Ende der Geschichte denkt Jojo, dass Sven mit ihr Schluss machen will. Sie und Lucilla lassen sich so einige Gründe einfallen, warum er nicht mehr mit ihr zusammen sein will. Welcher von den folgenden Gründen wird dabei *nicht* erwähnt?

- 1. He needs time to himself without Jojo.
- 2. He has found another girlfriend – or girlfriends!
- 3. He has been in a serious accident.
- 4. Jojo scared him off by wanting more romance.
- 5. Sven is having a secret affair with Lucilla.
- 6. He was worried by Jojo rubbing mayonnaise into his back.

## 5. Cross out

Sven hat nicht Schluss gemacht, aber Jojo leidet unter mangelndem Selbstbewusstsein. Streiche die Wörter durch, die Jojo nicht passend beschreiben.

confident ~~happy~~
nervous
~~sad~~
~~bold~~ flexible
unsure

All diese Wörter sind Adjektive – Adjektive beschreiben Personen und Gegenstände und bleiben im Englischen immer ohne Endung.

## 6. Fill in

In dieses Gespräch zwischen Jojo und Sven sind einige Wörter zuviel hineingeraten. Setze das passende Wort in die Lücke:

"You see, that's what I mean," I said. "That's not romantic; it's silly." Sven didn't seem too 1. _happy_    concerned    upset    happy

about that. "Then get me an

2. _instruction_ instruction    destruction    construction    manual

on being romantic, and I'll put on a bit of romance for you.

Do you want me to write you a

3. _poem_    play    poem    lovesong    or sing you a

4. _song_    solo    song    serenade    under your balcony?

Ignoring the fact that you don't actually have a balcony, of course."

### 7. Too many words!

In diesen Sätzen über Jojo und ihre Beziehung zu den anderen Familien-
mitgliedern fehlen Wörter. Fülle die Lücken mit den Wörtern aus der Box.
Aufgepasst: Es gibt mehr Wörter als Lücken! Streiche die überflüssigen
Wörter durch.

relaxing    annoying    ~~good~~    loves

dislikes    strange    difficult

~~biological~~    tricky    chemical

1. Although she __loves__ her very much, Jojo finds her little sister

   very __annoying__.

2. Jojo's mother finds it __difficult__ to leave Jojo alone in her room.

3. Although he is not her __biological__ father, Jojo and Oskar have a

   __good__ relationship.

## 8. Another odd one out

Jojos Mutter macht sich bei ihrer Tochter ständig zur Zielscheibe für deren Ärger: Kreuze an, über welche dieser Aktionen sich Jojo aufgeregt hat.

1. She sent Oskar up to Jojo's room with a cup of tea. ✓

2. She called Lucilla and asked her to be nice to Jojo. ✗

3. She offers to make her daughter a cup of tea and have a chat with her. ✗

4. She is in a good mood and comes and sits on Lucilla's bed.

> In der Gegenwart folgt auf he/she/it immer ein Verb mit s. In der Vergangenheit gibt es aber keins!

## 9. Correct the text

In diesem Text über Jojos Schwester Flippi haben sich 5 Fehler eingeschlichen. Finde und korrigiere sie. Die richtigen Wörter findest du auf der rechten Seite.

Jojo's ~~older~~ *younger* sister Flippi is ~~girlish~~ *boyish*.
She likes ~~fluffy~~ *slimy* animals such as snails.
She ~~always~~ *never* knocks before going into
Jojo's room and Jojo is ~~happy~~ *unhappy* about this.

> slimy
> ~~younger~~
> boyish
> unhappy
> ~~never~~

## 10. Crossword

Löse dieses Kreuzworträtsel! Fallen dir die Wörter nicht ein? Du findest sie in der Geschichte und den vorherigen Seiten.

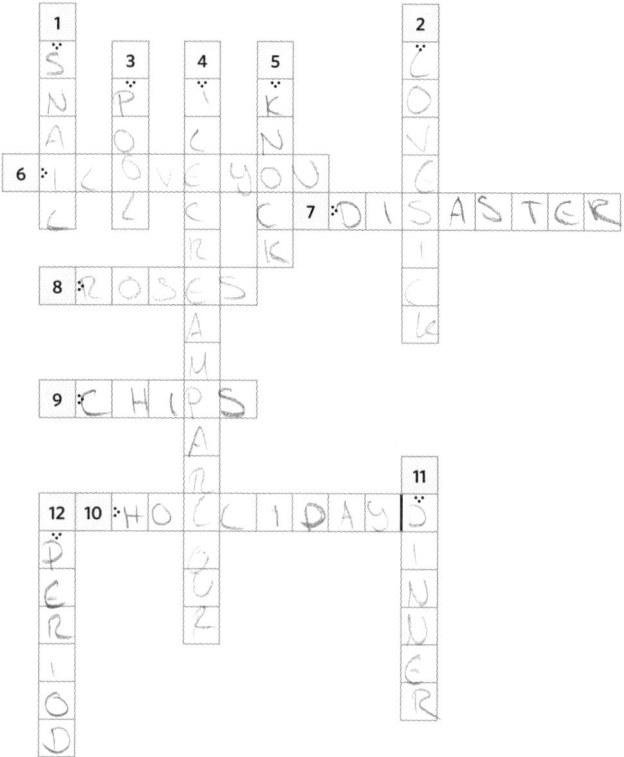

## ACROSS

6 This is what Sven wanted to tell Jojo after their meal together.

7 This is how Jojo describes her life at one point.

8 Sven makes a trail out of these in the park.

9 Sven and Jojo end up eating these.

10 The girls have a lot of free time because of these.

## DOWN

1 Flippi gives Jojo one of these.

2 Flippi calls her new breed of snail by this name.

3 Lucilla goes here, leaving Jojo alone in her room.

4 Sven is spotted here with two girls.

5 Flippi should do this before entering Jojo's room.

11 Oskar would invite a woman he loves to … what?

12 Maybe Sven just needs a Jojo-free … what?

## IV - ALL'S WELL THAT ENDS WELL

### 11. Save Sven's date!

Am Ende zeigt sich, dass Sven doch auf Jojos
Verlangen nach Romantik gehört hat: Nur weiß
er nicht, wie das geht. Er lässt sich also von
Freundinnen beraten, wie er den perfekten Abend
gestalten kann und schreibt dabei eine Liste. Leider
hat er in der Eisdiele Cola darüber gekippt. Findest du
heraus, welche Wörter verschwunden sind? Setze sie wieder ein.

> Diese Sätze sind alle in der Befehlsform geschrieben – diese Form ist im Englischen besonders einfach, da das Verb nicht konjugiert werden muss.

**1.** Buy a *cookery* book and plan a menu.

**2.** Get a long *table* and things to decorate it with –
e.g. rose petals, *candalable* , *serviettes* .

**3.** Take photos of myself with big *porcelain* to spell
out *I love you* .

**4.** Buy a bunch of *roses* to make a trail.

## 12. Multiple choice

A. Jojo bittet Lucilla, Sven zu folgen und ihr zu berichten, was er macht. Lucilla beobachtet, wie Sven in drei Geschäfte geht. Welche dieser Gegenstände hätte er für seinen romantischen Abend in den jeweiligen Geschäften besorgen können?

Flower shop: 1 _flowers_

Book shop: 2 _cookery book_

Supermarket: 3 _ingredients_,

4 _cutlery_,

5 _tablecloth_

cutlery

ingredients

flowers

cookery book

tablecloth

B. Wie heißen diese Gegenstände im Deutschen?

ingredients _Zutaten_

cutlery _Besteck_

flowers _Blumen_

cookery book _Kochbuch_

tablecloth _Tischdecke_

# The Football Pitch of Dreams

I - CHAOS THEORY, MAKE-UP AND WALLFLOWERS

## 1. Categorise

Die drei Mädchen in dieser Geschichte entsprechen alle völlig unterschiedlichen „Typen": Jojo, die Meisterin des Chaos; Lucilla, unbestrittene Mode-Königin und immer auf dem neuesten Stand und Sara, das zurückhaltende Mauerblümchen. Kannst du die englischen Wörter unten dem jeweiligen Charaktertypen zuordnen?

thoughtful    clumsy    hasty

quiet    cool    disorganised

stylish    shy    funky

| chaos queen | fashion girl | wallflower |
|---|---|---|
| disorganised | cool | shy |
| hasty | stylish | quit |
| clumsy | | thoughtful |

## 2. Connect

Verbinde nun die Charaktereigenschaften mit der passenden deutschen Übersetzung:

1. thoughtful
2. clumsy
3. hasty
4. shy
5. stylish
6. cool
7. quiet
8. disorganised
9. funky

6 A cool
3 B hastig
5 C modisch
7 D ruhig
1 E nachdenklich
2 F ungeschickt
4 G schüchtern
9 H flippig
8 I unorganisiert

## 3. Complete

In den folgenden Sätzen geht es um typisches Verhalten von Jojo, Lucilla und Sara - allerdings fehlt die zweite Hälfte. Obwohl alle drei Satzenden inhaltlich richtig sein könnten, gibt es nur eine Kombination, die in der Gesichte vorkommt. Kannst du für jeden Satz den richtigen Abschluss finden?

1. Lucilla is very interested in fashion so ...
- A she goes to the hairdresser every day.
- B she wants to be a model.
- C she always carries two T-shirts around in her bag.

> **"So"** erklärt hier eine Folge und wird im Deutschen am besten mit **also** oder **deswegen** übersetzt.

2. Jojo is known as the chaos queen and is so clumsy that she ...

  A is not allowed to go near the hotdog stand ever again.

  B falls over whenever she wears high-heeled shoes.

  C still does not know how to ride a bike.


3. Sara is not interested in fashion, which is why ...

  A she doesn't read girls' magazines.

  B Lucilla wants to give her a makeover.

  C she dislikes Lucilla.


## II - MAKEOVERS AND BEAUTY PAGEANTS

### 4. Fill in

In diesen Text über Saras „Verwandlung" sind einige Wörter zu viel hineingeraten. Streiche sie.


Lucilla starts by asking Sara whether she needs her 1 _glasses_

contact lenses/glasses/microscope to see. Sara says she cannot see very well

without them, but is happy to remove them. She is not happy about Lucilla

wanting to cut her 2 _hair_ hair/trousers/T-shirt. So Lucilla deci-

des to 3 _tie back_ layer/colour/tie back her hair and change Sara's 4

_shirt_ skirt/shirt/scarf from black to green. Then Lucilla finishes

off with matching 5 _make up_ shoes/make-up/hair.

## 5. Fetch

Lucilla kramt in ihrer Tasche herum: Sie sucht nach Make-up, damit sie Sara den letzten Feinschliff verpassen kann. Hilf ihr dabei, die Make-up-Utensilien herauszusuchen und streiche die Sachen durch, die sie in der Tasche liegen lassen kann.

lipstick    mascara    hand mirror
chewing gum
chocolate bar    facial cream    hairbrush
blusher    pencil

## 6. Find

In dieser Wortspirale sind einige Schönheitsutensilien und Kleidungsstücke verloren gegangen. Suche die Wörter wieder heraus.

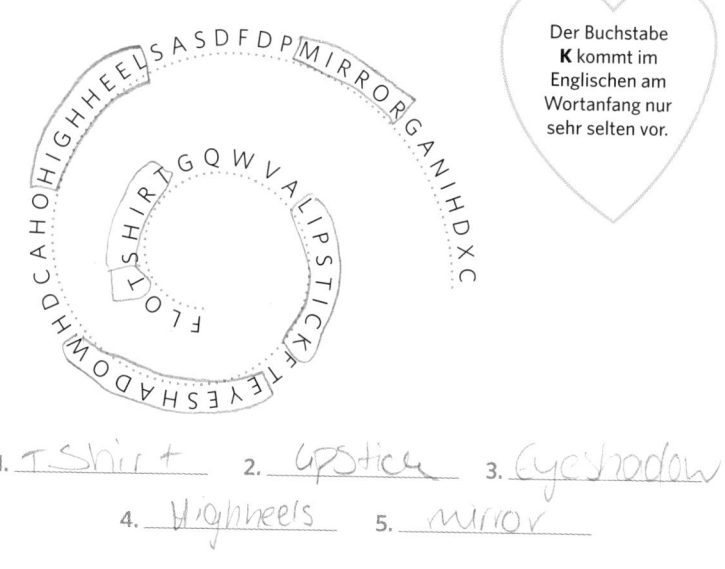

Der Buchstabe **K** kommt im Englischen am Wortanfang nur sehr selten vor.

1. T Shirt    2. Lipstick    3. Eyeshadow

4. Highheels    5. mirror

## 7. Odd one out

Lucillas Adlerauge bleibt nichts verborgen: zart aufkeimende Gefühle erkennt sie sofort - und hilft dem Glück auch gerne auf die Sprünge. Dass Sara Oliver kennen lernen möchte, hat sie dank einiger Signale gemerkt – welches aber war nicht dabei?

- 1. Sara keeps looking at Oliver while he's playing football.
- 2. Sara goes red when Oliver looks at her and then looks away.
- ✗ 3. Sara waves to Oliver when he looks at her.
- 4. Their eyes meet when Oliver goes to pick up the ball.

## 8. Too many words!

Lucilla erklärt Jojo, wie sie Sara und Oliver zusammenbringen will. Einige Wörter haben sich in die untenstehende Box verirrt. Fülle die Lücken - aber Achtung! Es gibt mehr Wörter als Lücken!

| | | | | | |
|---|---|---|---|---|---|
| fall | introduce | present | give | write | take |
| drop | meet | hit | say | disappear | |

1. First Jojo, you need to go and _introduce_ yourself to Oliver.

2. Then you'll need to get him to _meet_ us at the hotdog stand.

3. In the meantime, I'll _give_ Sara a makeover and _take_ her to the stand.

4. Then their eyes will meet and they'll _fall_ in love.

## 9. Anagram

Die Buchstaben in diesen Wörtern zum Thema „Verkuppeln" sind durcheinander geraten. Kannst du die Wörter wieder in Ordnung bringen?

1. T C H M A I N G M A K  *Matchmaking*
2. P I C U D  *Cupid*
3. O U C L P E  *couple*
4. S I T R F  T E D A  *First Date*

## IV - GEOGRAPHY OF THE SPORTS FIELD

## 10. Rearrange

Im untenstehenden Text wird die Sportanlage beschrieben. Leider sind die einzelnen Anlagen (= unterstrichene Wörter) in die falschen Sätze geraten und nichts steht mehr am richtigen Platz. Bringe die einzelnen Teile wieder an die richtige Stelle, indem du den richtigen Begriff über den falschen schreibst.

1. At the centre of the sports fields is the hot dog stand. *football pitch* Next to that there is an ice cream stand. *stand for spectators*

2. People who are hungry can go to either the stand for spectators *hot dog stand* or the changing rooms *ice cream stand* for refreshments.

3. The footballers get changed in the football pitch. *changing rooms*

120

### 11. Position

In diesem Text hat der Autor bestimmte Wörter vergessen. Hier sind einige Möglichkeiten zur Auswahl – wähle das richtige Wort und fülle die Lücken.

At the beginning of the story, Lucilla and Jojo are sitting _on_ 1

on/at/under the stand for spectators. Jojo has just been _at_ 2

in/on top of/at the hotdog stand. Then Jojo goes _to_ 3 at/on/to the

changing rooms and waits _outside_ 4 on top of/under/outside them. At the

end, Jojo and Lucilla listen to Sara and Oliver from 5 _behind_

behind/next to/in front of the ice-cream stand.

Wie lautet der grammatische Begriff für die 5 Wörter, die du soeben in die Lücken eingesetzt hast?

Präpositionen

# LÖSUNGEN

## Bliss Comes with a Kiss

I - MOVEMENTS OF LOVE AND PANIC

**1. Connect**
1A, 2D, 3C, 4B, 5E

**2. Translate**
1. plötzlich auf der Stelle stehen bleiben
2. jemanden am Arm packen
3. tief Luft holen
4. die Tür zuknallen
5. die Bettdecke über den Kopf ziehen

**3. Complete**
1B, 2A, 3C

II - WHY WOULD HE BREAK UP WITH ME?

**4. Out one out**
5.

**5. Cross out**
confident, happy, bold, flexible

**6. Fill in**
1. happy, 2. instruction, 3. poem, 4. serenade

III - YOU CAN CHOOSE YOUR FRIENDS, BUT NOT YOUR FAMILY!

**7. Too many words!**
1. loves, annoying, 2. difficult, 3. biological, good

**8. Another odd one out**
2, 3, 4 – über 1. hat sich Jojo in der Tat gefreut

**9. Correct the text**
Jojo's *younger* sister Flippi is *boyish*. She likes *slimy* animals such as snails. She *never* knocks before going into Jojo's room and Jojo is *unhappy* about this.

### 10. Crossword

Across: 6. I love you, 7. disaster, 8. roses, 9. chips, 10. holidays
Down: 1. snail, 2. love-sick, 3. pool, 4. ice-cream parlour, 5. knock,
11. dinner, 12. period

..................................................................

## IV. ALL'S WELL THAT ENDS WELL

### 11. Save Sven's date!

1. cookery, 2. table, candelabra, serviettes, porcelain (mehrere Antworten möglich),
3. letters, I love you, 4. roses

### 12. Multiple choice

A.
Flower shop: flowers
Book shop: cookery book
Supermarket: ingredients, cutlery, tablecloth

B.
Zutaten, Besteck, Blumen, Kochbuch, Tischdecke

..................................................................

## ANTWORTEN ZU DEN "LOVE-QUESTIONS"

1.
No babe, I'm not angry at u
but it was a silly idea!

*Jojo antwortet, dass sie nicht böse ist. Aber die Idee, dass Sven bei einem Unfall schwer verletzt worden sein soll, war schon sehr blöd.*

2.
How should I feel? No I
didn't talk to my mum! U
know I don't talk 2 her
about my problems!

*Jojo schreibt zurück, dass sie sich mit ihrer Mutter über die „Sven-Situation" nicht unterhalten hat. Wenn irgendwie möglich, versucht sie solche Themen mit ihrer Mutter zu vermeiden ... und wie soll sie sich wohl fühlen?*

3.
No I haven't called Sven.
He should call me!

*Jojo ist der Meinung, Sven solle sie anrufen und nicht umgekehrt. Daher hat sie sich (noch) nicht bei ihm gemeldet.*

```
4.
Yes, Sven called but I
didn't answer. He wants
me 2 meet him at the park
tomorrow!
```

*Sven hat sich bei Jojo gemeldet, aber sie ist nicht ans Telefon gegangen. Ihre Schwester Flippi richtet ihr aus, Sven wolle sich am nächsten Tag mit ihr im Park treffen.*

```
5.
Hi Lu! Wow! It was really
romantic! He made me a
picnic in the park! :-)
```

*Jojo hat Tolles zu berichten: Sie hatte ein wahnsinnig romantisches Date im Park mit Sven und alles ist wieder in Ordnung!*

# The Football Pitch of Dreams

........................................................................

## I - CHAOS THEORY, MAKE-UP AND WALLFLOWERS

**1. Categorise**
chaos queen: disorganised, hasty, clumsy
fashion girl: cool, stylish
Wallflower: quiet, shy, thoughtful

**2. Connect**
1E, 2F, 3B, 4G, 5C, 6A, 7D, 8I, 9H

**3. Complete**
1C, 2A, 3B

........................................................................

## II - MAKEOVERS AND BEAUTY PAGEANTS

**4. Fill in**
1. glasses, 2. hair, 3. tie back, 4. shirt, 5. make-up

**5. Fetch**
Durchgestrichen: chewing gum, chocolate bar, hairbrush, pencil

**6. Find**
1. T-shirt, 2. lipstick, 3. eye-shadow
4. high heels, 5. mirror

........................................................................

## III - MATCHMAKING: NOT AS EASY AS IT LOOKS

**7. Odd one out**
3 - Sara waves to Oliver when he looks at her.

**8. Too many words**
1. introduce, 2. meet, 3. give, take, 4. fall

**9. Anagram**
1. MATCHMAKING
2. CUPID
3. COUPLE
4. FIRST DATE

**10. Rearrange**
1. At the centre of the sports fields is the <u>football pitch</u>.
   Next to that there is a <u>stand for spectators</u>.
2. People who are hungry can go to either the
   <u>hotdog stand</u> or the <u>ice-cream stand</u> for refreshments.
3. The footballers get changed in the <u>changing rooms</u>.

> Hast du bei 1.
> darauf geachtet,
> den unbestimm-
> ten Artikel
> von **an** zu **a** zu
> ändern?

**11. Position**
A 1. on, 2. at, 3. to, 4. outside, 5. behind
B Alle Wörter sind Präpositionen.

. . . . . . . . . . . . . . . . . . . . . . . . . . . . . . . . . . . . . . . . . . . . . . . . . . . . . . .

ANTWORTEN ZU DEN "LOVE-QUESTIONS"

1.
I'm at the changing rooms,
w8ting 4 Olli 2 come out!
xx

*Jojo antwortet, dass sie vor den Umkleidekabinen auf Olli wartet. Was ganz schön lange dauert ...*

2.
Ur a hero! Sara is in a bad
mood as always :P

*Lucilla, die gerade mit Sara beschäftigt ist, gibt Jojo zu verstehen, dass diese eine gute Tat vollbringt ... und Sara ist schlecht gelaunt wie immer.*

3.
Lu, we r on our way 2 u
right now! I found Olli
+ am bringing him 2 the
stand.

*Jojo meldet, dass sie Olli gefunden hat und mit ihm unterwegs zum Hotdog-Stand ist. Die Umstände der Begegnung behält sie lieber erst einmal für sich.*

# Freches Englisch mit den Frechen Mädchen

Hier dreht sich alles um die kleinen Missverständnisse zwischen Jungs und Mädchen, die Tücken der Pubertät und den ganz alltäglichen Wahnsinn mit Eltern, Geschwistern und Freundinnen.
So könnt Ihr mit den frechen Büchern ganz nebenbei Euren englischen Wortschatz erweitern und Eure Grammatikkenntnisse verbessern. Alle Lovestories auch zum Anhören auf MP3-CD.

**Alle Bände aus einer Reihe:**

*Kisses, Cuddles & Holiday Love*
**ISBN:** 978-3-12-010022-5

*Love, Twists & Blissful Kisses*
**ISBN:** 978-3-12-010023-2

*Flirting, Fun & Chaotic Kisses*
**ISBN:** 978-3-12-010021-8

www.pons.de